Living the Word

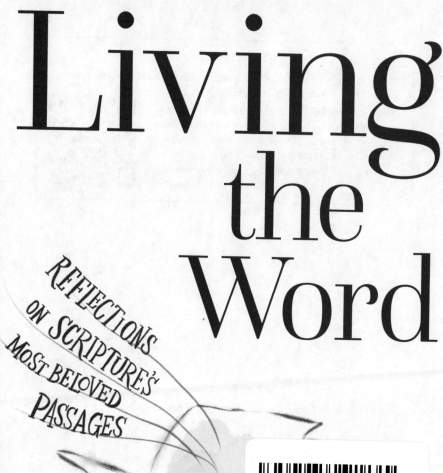

REFLECTIONS ON SCRIPTURE'S MOST BELOVED PASSAGES

EDITORS *of* GUIDEPOSTS

A Gift from Guideposts

Thank you for your purchase! We want to express our gratitude for your support with a special gift just for you.

Dive into *Spirit Lifters*, a complimentary e-book that will fortify your faith, offering solace during challenging moments. Its 31 carefully selected scripture verses will soothe and uplift your soul.

Please use the QR code or go to **guideposts.org/spiritlifters** to download.

Living the Word: Reflections on Scripture's Most Beloved Passages

Published by Guideposts
100 Reserve Rd., Suite E200
Danbury, CT 06810
Guideposts.org

Copyright © 2025 Guideposts. All rights reserved.

This book, or parts thereof, may not be reproduced, stored in a retrieval system, or transmitted in any form or by any means, electronic, mechanical, photocopying, recording, or otherwise, without the written permission of the publisher.
Cover design by Kristi Smith, Juicebox Designs
Typeset by Aptara, Inc.

ISBN 978-1-961442-44-3 (softcover)
ISBN 978-1-961442-45-0 (epub)

Printed and bound in the United States of America
10 9 8 7 6 5 4 3 2 1

Contents

Introduction	3
Do Not Worry—Matthew 6:34	8
Ten-Finger Rule—Philippians 4:13	12
Time for Every Purpose under Heaven—Ecclesiastes 3:1–8	16
Be Still—Psalm 46:10	21
God's Right Hand—Isaiah 41:10	25
Small Beginnings—Zechariah 4:10	29
Caregiving—John 19:26–27	33
What's in a Word?—Joshua 22:5	37
Sit Quietly with Me—Job 2:11–13	41
Even If—Daniel 3:16–18	45
Think about Such Things—Philippians 4:8	50
God Is My Refuge—Psalm 91:1–2	54
God the Singer—Zephaniah 3:17	58
Home Sweet Home—John 14:1–3	62
Hope and a Future—Jeremiah 29:11	66
Hemmed In—Psalm 139:5	70
I Am Chosen and I Belong—Isaiah 43:1	74
What Lies Ahead—Philippians 3:13–14	78
Keep Your Eyes on God—2 Chronicles 20:12	82
I Will Not Leave You Desolate—John 14:18–19	87
Digging Wells of Blessings—Psalm 84:5–6	92
Living in Light of Eternity—Ecclesiastes 3:11	96
To Whom Shall We Go?—John 6:66–69	100
The Greatest of These—1 Corinthians 13:13	104

Earnestly Seeking God—Psalm 63:1–8	108
Loving Your Neighbor—Matthew 22:36–40	113
The A-Team—Ephesians 3:20–21	117
Cast Your Cares on Him—1 Peter 5:7	121
Nothing Can Separate Us—Romans 8:38–39	125
In God's Time—Psalm 138:8	129
Prayers for Comfort—2 Corinthians 1:3–4	133
Redefining My Identity—Luke 7:47	138
Remain in Me—John 15:4	142
Stumbling but Not Falling—Psalm 46:5	146
Surrender in Suffering—Romans 5:3–5	150
The Beauty and Power of Lament—Psalm 13	154
The Lord Will Fight for You—Exodus 14:14	158
An Open Door—Revelation 3:7	162
The Solid, Immutable Rock—Hebrews 13:8	167
Overflowing with Assurance—Romans 15:13	171
A Spirit of Youth—Psalm 103:1–5	175
Trading Anxiety for His Peace—John 14:27	179
Wearing God's Word—Isaiah 43:1–2	183
Content with Weakness—2 Corinthians 12:9–10	188
Finding Safety—Psalm 121	193
Where the Good Is—Jeremiah 6:16	197
Where Your Treasure Is—Matthew 6:19, 21	201
Wisdom for Senior Living—Psalm 90:12	205
Writing on His Hand—Isaiah 44:1–5	209
A Mom Next Door—Psalm 68:6	213
Acknowledgments	217
A Note from the Editors	219

Introduction

HEATHER JEPSEN

In the beginning was the Word, and the Word was with God, and the Word was God.

—John 1:1, NIV

Many will recognize this verse as the beginning of the Gospel of John. Unlike some of our other Gospels that begin with the story of Jesus's birth, this Gospel writer pans way back with his lens, opening on a cosmic scene. Before all time there was the Word, and this Word was God.

Over time we have come to understand that the Gospel writer is talking about Jesus Christ. Jesus existed before time, and Jesus most clearly defines for us who God is and who God calls us to be. When we dig deeper into the original language of the New Testament, we discover that what is translated as *Word* is *Logos* in Greek. *Logos* can also be translated as *conversation*. What would it mean to read, "In the beginning was the conversation"? All of creation is in conversation, and Jesus is the epitome of God's conversation with humanity. Scripture offers us the gift of being in conversation with God.

When we consider the Word of God today, we think of both Jesus and our Bible as a whole. The Bible is God's Word to us, and the Bible is a conversation. It is a record of God's people and their triumphs and struggles. Through its arc we can trace the story of God's love. From the creation of Adam and Eve through the story of the nation of Israel, from the accounts of Jesus to the days of the early church, the Bible is God's conversation with us. The Bible is the gift of God's Word to uplift and inspire.

When King David was writing psalms, he mused on the Word of God.

> The law of the LORD is perfect, refreshing the soul. The statutes of the LORD are trustworthy, making wise the simple. The precepts of the LORD are right, giving joy to the heart. The commands of the LORD are radiant, giving light to the eyes. The fear of the LORD is pure, enduring forever. The decrees of the LORD are firm, and all of them are righteous. They are more precious than gold, than much pure gold; they are sweeter than honey, than honey from the honeycomb. By them your servant is warned; in keeping them there is great reward. (Psalm 19:7–11, NIV)

Sweeter than honey from the honeycomb—what a powerful image of the goodness of God's Word for us!

As a pastor, I spend a lot of time immersed in scripture. Every week I prepare a new sermon and look for fresh ways to apply the stories and lessons from the Bible to our daily lives. We talk about the Bible as the living Word of God, and it never fails to amaze me how the texts have changed and transformed me and my thinking throughout the years. The words, of course, are the same as they have been for centuries, but their meaning changes as I grow older and the circumstances of our world change.

When I preach on a scripture passage that I have preached on before, I sometimes look back at other sermons I have written. I am often surprised that a past sermon's direction is so different from where I feel I am heading with a text today. The Word of God is alive. Some years I hear one message for my congregation; other years I will discover something completely different from the same story. The Word of God is dynamic, offering us fresh insights as we move through our lives. The Bible offers us wisdom that we can apply to our unique situation and circumstances every day.

Just as we can always find new messages within it, the Word of God is also always steady. Jesus tells us, "Everyone who hears these words of mine and puts them into practice is like a wise man who built his house on the rock. The rain came down, the streams rose, and the winds blew and beat against that house; yet it did not fall, because it had its foundation on the rock. But everyone who hears these words of mine and does not put them into practice is like a foolish man who built his house on sand. The rain came down, the streams rose, and the winds blew and beat against that house, and it fell with a great crash" (Matthew 7:24–27, NIV).

The Word of God is steady and solid like a rock. It is something we can count on to lead us throughout our whole lives. While our circumstances may change, some scriptures will always apply, and returning to them over and over feels like coming home. When I read, "The LORD is my shepherd" (Psalm 23:1, NIV)—even if I am reading it for the hundredth or thousandth time—I'm reminded of how God desires to protect me and guide me, as a shepherd, to a better way of life.

The Word of God is of infinite value. Jesus tells us, "Heaven and earth will pass away, but my words will never pass away" (Matthew 24:35, NIV). What other book have people read over and over again for thousands of years and still continue to find fresh meaning and insight? That we have access to such a wonder is truly a gift of God.

In your hands today you hold a treasure. Writers have shared their favorite passages of scripture, and they tell stories of how those verses have affected their lives. These are words that have helped folks through some of their darkest hours. These are words that have helped friends discover new meaning in difficult circumstances. These are words that have provided hope and encouragement for all humanity.

If you are looking for a new way to connect with God, you have come to the right place. In reading these stories, you, too, will be inspired to connect with the Word of God in a deeply personal way. Each of these authors has included a Faith Step at the end of their story that offers practical encouragement for seeking God anew each day. Full of insight and suggestions that inspire, these authors give practical advice for things you can do today that will change your life tomorrow.

I did not grow up in the church, so I know what it is like to live without a grounding in the stories of God and God's people. When I was young, I floated along through life without a sense of purpose or belonging. I felt untethered and ungrounded, as if any little thing could blow me away.

When I came to the faith, I began to immerse myself in scripture. I had never read the Bible before, so I started there. Yes, it was a task to read it from beginning to end, but it was worth the effort. When we sit and read the Bible like we would any other book, we are exposed to the great scope of God's message and God's love for creation.

Eventually I began to take the words of scripture to heart, memorizing them and seeking their meaning for my life. It is that kind of knowing that you will read about in this volume. Some verses just stick with us, guiding us, offering us hope, reminding us of God's love for us.

Reading this volume, as well as other offerings from Guideposts, is a great way to begin your own journey with the Word of God. If you would like to dig deeper, there are a wide variety of resources available. But I would also recommend returning to scripture itself. Keep a Bible by your bedside and read a psalm every night. This is a great place to begin, as the

Psalms are the prayers and songs of the early people of God. In the Psalms we find both joy and lament.

If you have a bit of time, another idea is to sit down and read one of the Gospels (Matthew, Mark, Luke, and John) in one sitting as if you were reading a novel. When we do this, we get a unique perspective on the life and message of Jesus Christ. The Gospels are all different in their tone and method of storytelling, and each one provides a unique portrait of our Savior. Challenge yourself to read all four and consider which image of Christ resonates most with you.

The Bible is a gift of infinite depth and breadth from God to believers of all walks of life. It has a general message that is for all people (the love of God), and it also has a way of speaking to each one of us individually. The Bible is a doorway into that conversation with God. Where is God leading you in your life? Who is God calling you to be? The Bible is the starting point for those conversations.

My friends, every day is a unique opportunity to experience the Word of God in your life. This volume from Guideposts offers stories from ordinary people about how the Word of God has made extraordinary impacts in their lives. You, too, can discover the wonders of God's Word. I pray that as you read this volume, your eyes are opened, your heart is warmed, and you are inspired to begin (or continue) your own journey with God's Word. "In the beginning was the Word, and the Word was with God, and the Word was God" (John 1:1, NIV). Welcome to the conversation!

Do Not Worry

JENNIE IVEY

Take therefore no thought for the morrow: for the morrow shall take thought for the things of itself. Sufficient unto the day is the evil thereof.

—Matthew 6:34, KJV

I come from a long line of worriers, beginning with my mother and going back generations. Mother grew up during the Great Depression and World War II and, like many of her contemporaries, never completely stopped worrying about having "enough." Enough food. Enough clothes. Enough heat. Enough gasoline. And on and on and on.

By the time my siblings and I came along, she'd learned to keep most of those anxieties to herself. Anytime we expressed worry about something, Mother would say, "Sufficient unto the day is the evil thereof."

I was about five years old the first time she said it to me. "What does that mean?" I asked.

"It's from the Bible," she told me. "Jesus said it. It's a fancy way of saying don't worry."

"Ah," I said, nodding my head.

I try to live by those words. But, as in many of the things Jesus asks of us, it's easier said than done. As a child and teenager, I worried about grades and sports and best friends and boyfriends. I grew up and had kids of my own and worried about them. Was I feeding them right? Was it OK for them to ride bicycles in the street, or should they stay on the driveway? Would they need braces? Could we afford braces? Was I helping enough with homework? Helping too much with homework?

Naturally, the worries got bigger when they became teenagers. Were they hanging out with the right kind of friends? Would they say no to alcohol and drugs? And how could I bear the thought of them driving a car?

Thankfully, they grew up just fine and have spouses and children of their own. Meaning I now have two generations behind me to worry about.

My husband of thirty-five years and I divorced when we were in our early sixties. I was filled with pain and consumed with new worries. There were times when I felt I would never again have a stress-free day or a solid night's sleep. A decade has passed since then, and I'm generally OK during the day. But nights are often difficult. It's hard to fall asleep and hard to stay asleep. And not just because the icemaker drops a load of cubes into the bin or my next-door neighbor fires up his noisy pickup truck just as I'm nodding off.

Many nights, my brain just won't shut down. Sometimes, it's filled with random crazy questions. How, exactly, does the moon affect the tides? If I went back to high school now, would algebra be harder or easier? Is sleet the same thing as freezing rain? Am I too old to learn to play the piano? Does anybody actually gather walnuts anymore and try to get to the meat? What, exactly, is the difference between Great Britain and the United Kingdom?

Mostly, though, my mind is filled with worries. Little worries, like how to keep squirrels off my bird feeder and trumpet vine out of my hydrangeas. Is it time to schedule a tire rotation for my car? When did I last change the furnace filter? Will the birthday card I sent to my friend get to her in time (because we all know how the mail is these days)?

But many of my worries are about big stuff. Will I need hip replacement? Knee replacement? A coronary bypass? How much longer will my fifteen-year-old car make it? Do I have snakes in my attic? Is that better or worse than having mice in my attic? And what will I do if a snake or a mouse gets out of the attic and into my bedroom? Do the deer grazing in my yard have tick-borne diseases? Will I catch those diseases if I walk barefoot through the grass? What will I do if I lose my cell phone? What will I do if someone breaks into my house while I'm away? What will I do if someone breaks into my house while I'm home? If my dog dies before I do, how will I bury her? (She's big and I'm not a good digger.)

And there are the same old worries about my grandkids that I had about my own kids: health, school, friends, riding bicycles, driving cars.

Let's not forget gigantic worries about the whole wide world. War and pestilence. Fires and floods. Tornadoes and tsunamis. The news breaks my heart every single day. But as a citizen of Planet Earth, I feel it's my duty to stay informed.

I try to do all the "right" things when it comes to sleep. Turning off screens—TV, phone, and tablet—at least an hour before bedtime. A warm bath. A mug of herbal tea. A comfortable pillow. A cool, dark bedroom. I snuggle beneath the covers and say my prayers, confident I have eight hours of solid sleep ahead of me. Almost immediately, my mind begins to whir. The white noise of the floor fan in the corner of my room doesn't help. Nor does playing soothing sounds—ocean waves, frogs and crickets, rain falling—on my phone. Lullabies don't help, either.

I try other tricks. Relaxing my muscles, beginning with my toes and working my way up to my neck. Relaxing my muscles going in the opposite direction. Singing the ABC song forward. Singing it backward. I picture myself in a beautiful meadow, listening to birds sing, watching butterflies flit about, and romping around with an entire litter of adorable puppies. Even that seldom works.

And then I remember what Jesus said: *Do not worry.* Sometimes whispering those three words over and over again lulls me to sleep.

When it doesn't, I reach back into my memory for the entire verse from Matthew 6:34, the one in the King James edition. I remember standing in the sunny kitchen with my mother when I was only five years old, talking about something that was worrying me. And I hear Mother's gentle voice recite these ancient words of comfort: "Take therefore no thought for the morrow: for the morrow shall take thought for the things of itself. Sufficient unto the day is the evil thereof."

Almost always, my eyelids grow heavy and I fall into a deep and restful sleep.

Faith Step

List your worries on paper. All of them. Then, at the top of the page—in all capital letters—write Jesus's words: DO NOT WORRY. Keep the list handy so you can refer to it when necessary.

Ten-Finger Rule

ANNE FOLEY RAUTH

I can do all things through Christ who strengthens me.

—Philippians 4:13, NKJV

I didn't know much about soccer when our oldest son, Benjamin, started playing for his small Christian middle school. The good news: At a smaller school, everyone gets playing time (PT for short). The bad news: You might get called up for a position you've never played before at, quite literally, a moment's notice.

That's exactly what happened when Benjamin's team faced their rival school. The boy who had been playing goalie left the team, and because Benjamin was one of the taller and older boys, he was selected to step into the role. Minutes before the game, he was handed the goalie gloves and was told, "You're up." I was stunned to see him donning the goalie's special shirt and jogging out to the opposite end of the field.

Goalie, I later learned, is arguably the most important position on the team—responsible for stopping every shot and rallying the defense. Benjamin had no training or experience for this position, and I knew he needed encouragement—and fast. Not only from his family and friends on the sidelines but also from above. As the game began, I found myself silently praying, while also shouting words of encouragement from the sidelines as any former cheerleader should. "You're doing great, Ben," I said over and over, as I continued my silent petitions.

It was a brutal game. Our team was young and inexperienced and didn't score a single goal. Benjamin, as the new goalie, was kept constantly busy defending the net against a high-scoring team. For his first game, I was proud to see that he did stop several goals. Even so, many also made their way through his gloves and into the net. As the final whistle blew, our team was defeated, and Benjamin, especially, looked crushed.

When the teams lined up to shake one another's hands at the end of the game, several members of the opposing team insulted Benjamin, saying, "You're the worst goalie we've ever played against," and "Where did they find you to play goalie?"

Benjamin was devastated, and I could see in my rearview mirror as we drove home that he was choked up and holding back tears. Even the usual treat to stop for ice cream was rejected, leaving his two younger brothers disappointed as well.

"Benjamin, I believe in you," I said softly. "And, more importantly, God believes in you, and we're going to figure this out." My words rang hollow as he went to his room, announcing he never wanted to play soccer again.

That night, as I thought and prayed about the situation, a quote from St. Augustine came to mind: "Pray as if everything depended on God. Work as if everything depended on you." Taking that advice to heart, I decided to do a little work. My high school and college didn't have soccer teams, so my knowledge was limited. But I knew it was about time to learn. I prayed for guidance and reached out to my network asking if anyone knew of a "goalie coach." (I didn't even know if such a thing existed, but I figured it couldn't hurt to ask.)

To my surprise, a friend connected me with a woman who had been a goalie in college and was willing to coach Benjamin. She told me she could help him not only improve his goalie skills but also gain confidence as an overall soccer player. I still remember one of the first lessons she taught him: "Benjamin, even the goalie can score a goal!" She recognized that he had a strong kick and wanted him to know that goalies had power and the potential to score.

With the new coach in place, we had the work part in motion, but we also needed to combine that with the prayer part. One of my favorite verses, which seemed to match our current situation, is Philippians 4:13: "I can do all things through Christ who strengthens me." Though an encouraging verse, it clearly was too long to shout from the sidelines.

One day as I thought about how I could encourage Ben during soccer games, I looked down at my hands and noticed that I have ten fingers. There are also ten words in Philippians 4:13. One word for each finger. Suddenly, I had my cheer, and the Ten-Finger Rule was born!

"Ben," I said, "I'm going to yell something from the sideline, and it's going to be a special signal just between you and me. I'm going to yell, 'Ten-Finger Rule' and hold up both my hands so you can see them. That's your reminder that you can do all things through Christ who strengthens you."

"Deal," he replied with a small smile.

We had a goalie coach. We had prayers going up. We had our special cheer. Time for the next game.

It wasn't as rough as the first one, but our team didn't win. However, the goalie looked much more confident in the net. Whenever Benjamin needed encouragement, I would yell, "Ten-Finger Rule" from the sideline and hold up all ten fingers. Ben would raise his gloved hands in return, sending the secret signal back, and I could see a renewed focus on his face.

After that game, Benjamin seemed a bit more encouraged and even excited to keep practicing with the coach. The next time they met, she reminded him that the goalie is the commander on the field. "You're not just blocking shots, Benjamin," she said. "You're directing the defense, coordinating the team. You run the show."

At the next game, Benjamin started yelling instructions to everyone on the team, including his middle brother, and the action started to happen. Miraculously, we won a game! I could see that his leadership skills were blossoming, and his teammates responded to his guidance, playing with more unity and energy.

Over the years, as Ben played throughout middle school and high school, I witnessed an incredible transformation. He had poise, gained confidence, and became the commander of each soccer team that he played for. I loved watching him play soccer, and his love for the game continued to grow each season. I cherished each game and each time I yelled, "Ten-Finger Rule!"

That goalie may not be playing soccer now, but when I text or tell him, "Ten-Finger Rule," he immediately knows: Philippians 4:13. Short enough to shout from the sidelines and powerful enough for a child to remember who ultimately has his back and where his strength comes from.

Words to play by. Words to live by.

Faith Step

Incorporating scripture into everyday life is a great way to live out your faith. Choose a scripture that you can abbreviate and use with your family during stressful situations or times when you need extra encouragement.

Time for Every Purpose under Heaven

JESSICA ANDRUS LINDSTROM

To everything there is a season, a time for every purpose under heaven: a time to be born, and a time to die; a time to plant, and a time to pluck what is planted; a time to kill, and a time to heal; a time to break down, and a time to build up; a time to weep, and a time to laugh; a time to mourn, and a time to dance; a time to cast away stones, and a time to gather stones; a time to embrace, and a time to refrain from embracing; a time to gain, and a time to lose; a time to keep, and a time to throw away; a time to tear, and a time to sew; a time to keep silence, and a time to speak; a time to love, and a time to hate; a time of war, and a time of peace.

—Ecclesiastes 3:1–8, NKJV

Standing at the window of our cottage on Lake Michigan, I watched the undulating waves washing onto shore. My hand, placed on my bulging belly, felt the movements of my baby within. My husband was miles away, working in Wyoming.

"Oh, Lord," I whispered. "Have I done the right thing?"

It had been my choice to stay behind when Tim got his new job. After months of turmoil, I needed some semblance of order and stability, especially for our son, Carl, who had just started school. I asked God for courage to face the coming months. I prayed for peace of mind.

Just fifteen months before, we'd been happily renovating our farmhouse in Virginia. Pregnant with another child, I was working from home as a writer for a foundation and enjoying the time spent raising our three-year-old son. And then, almost overnight, our life turned upside down.

First, I lost my job. Shortly thereafter, Tim responded to an emergency call from Michigan. His father, still living independently with his bedridden wife, had fallen. Tim drove thirteen hours to his childhood home, arranged for the medical transport of his parents to Virginia, and, after seeing them off at the airport, drove back with their belongings and pets—two cats and a large dog—packed into our station wagon. At home, I rearranged rooms, preparing for my in-laws' arrival. Our son danced around in excitement.

"Grandpa and Grandma are coming to live with us," he sang. "And so are the kitties, Suki and Sam, and Molly, the collie!"

Part of our renovations included a new guest room, which was roughed in enough for the placement of a bed, bureau, and chair for my father-in-law. Together, Carl and I arranged flowers in a vase and placed them on the bureau.

"Grandpa will love them!" Carl crooned.

Downstairs in our living area, a medical bed had been delivered for my mother-in-law, and a nurse had arrived to help with her transfer and oversee my training as her new primary caregiver.

Carl saw flashing lights through the window as an ambulance drove up the drive. "Grandma and Grandpa are here!" he shouted with glee.

To our surprise and utter dismay, the medics transferred only Grandma into the house. There was something wrong with Grandpa; he was delirious and in pain. The medics drove him to the ER. Two days later, Tim arrived, just in time to sit by his father's side before he died.

I knew now why the loss of my job was a preordained blessing. I had much work to do—not only caring for and consoling

Carl but also bathing his Grandma Jane, feeding her through her G-tube, changing her colostomy bag, and administering her medications. Although it was difficult for her to talk, Jane was able to communicate in writing, and we spent many hours conversing on yellow legal pads. She mourned the unexpected loss of her husband but expressed anticipatory joy for the arrival of a new grandchild.

"I hope it will be a girl," she wrote.

Two weeks later, those hopes crumbled. A sonogram revealed the developing child within me was dying. At twenty-one weeks, his heart stopped.

Oh, God, give me the strength to go on, I prayed.

It was at that time Jane requested an advanced directive. She made it very clear that she did not want to be resuscitated if her heart stopped or if she ceased breathing. We promised to do her will. But God had other plans.

A nurse, whom my husband and I had hired to sit with Jane overnight while we slept, was with her when Jane aspirated and became unconscious one night. The nurse had already called 911 before awakening us, and the EMT crew immediately performed CPR and transported her to the ER.

When Tim and I entered Jane's hospital room the next morning, she was awake and angry. Her narrowed eyes communicated her thoughts: "How could you have resuscitated me against my will?"

"I'm sorry," Tim said gently. "But God must have plans for you that we don't know about or understand."

"Like having you here with us today to celebrate Carl's birthday," I added softly. Jane's face brightened, and she smiled.

Later that morning, from her hospice bed, she watched with delight as her grandson unwrapped his presents, blew out his four candles, and devoured his cake.

"Happy birthday to me!" he squealed at the top of his voice, spinning around the room like a toy top.

I scolded him sternly and then felt strong fingers clutching my arm. Turning, I saw Jane distinctly mouthing the words: "Leave him alone!"

Then an inspiration hit me. "Jane," I said, turning to her again. "Do you want to be baptized?"

Tim's parents hadn't been very religious, but they had baptized him and taken him to Sunday school while he was growing up. Jane's parents had never taken her to church. Nor had they baptized any of their three children.

"Do you want to be baptized?" I repeated.

Jane's eyes shone. She nodded yes.

That afternoon a priest from our church arrived with a Bible, the prayer book, a candle, and holy water and oil in hand. The three of us stood as witnesses while the priest performed the holy sacrament. Carl helped light the baptismal candle at the ceremony's end. I remember tears of joy.

That evening Jane slipped into a coma. She died the following day.

We were not left with much time to mourn. Shortly after the funeral, Tim learned that his job no longer existed. In a flurry, we put our farmhouse on the market, drove to Michigan to sell his parents' home, and then returned to pack up our belongings and move to a small cottage on Lake Michigan, a summer vacation residence Tim's parents had built when he was a child. After installing insulation, a washing machine, and baseboard heating—in addition to transporting the bulk of our belongings to a local storage unit—we moved into the cottage and regrouped. So much had happened. It seemed we were rejoicing only to mourn; building up only to tear things down; finding our way, only to lose it again.

The fluttering movements of the baby inside me brought me back to the present. It was almost time to greet the school bus that would bring Carl home from kindergarten.

That night we would call Tim to tell him about our day and to ask him about his. Once the baby was born and the school year had ended, we would drive together to our new home in the Rockies. The move would be yet another step of faith in the many we had made over the past fifteen months, believing God had plans for us even when we could not fathom what they were. Soon the baby girl Jane had wished for would arrive—a time for weeping would be supplanted by laughter, and the expectations God had for our futures would unfold.

"Thank You, Lord," I spoke aloud. "Thank You for these gifts—these seasons of our life."

Faith Step

Have you experienced a setback recently or the loss of a loved one? Offer up your sorrows to God. Pray for renewal and peace. Know that the dark days will become bright again through Jesus's healing power and God's divine grace.

Be Still

HEATHER JEPSEN

He says, "Be still, and know that I am God."

—Psalm 46:10, NIV

I awake with a start at 5:30 a.m. Once again, the day is upon me, and even though the sun has yet to grace the sky, I have tasks that need to get done. I take a quick shower and head downstairs to feed my pets. Once all pets have eaten and gone outside, I start on myself. As I cook my eggs, I check the clock. My son still is not out of bed, so I go upstairs to pester him.

I hate getting my son up for school. He's grumpy, I'm grumpy, and by 6:30 in the morning we risk being late. After a bit of yelling, he gets up and comes downstairs to make himself something to eat. By 6:55 a.m., we are out the door. I drop him at the middle school, drive back home, get my daughter, and drop her at the high school by 7:15 a.m.

Back home, I can finally breathe. I leash up the dogs and head out for our walk. Now my favorite time of the day begins. Together the dogs and I stroll, enjoying the sights, sounds, and smells of a fresh new day. "Be still," I remind myself. Don't get too caught up in the hustle and bustle. This day is in God's hands.

When we get back home, I clean the kitchen. As I look out the window, my stained glass hanging sign reminds me, "Be still, and know that I am God." I get dressed for work and head off to the church for a busy day of ministry.

I am a pastor, and I love my job. I love that it is my job to read scripture, to write sermons, to study God's Word, and to wonder what the message is for the day. However, my job requires much more of me than that.

"Heather, come downstairs," I hear over my intercom. "Someone is here to see you." Interrupted, I go downstairs to find an angry parishioner.

"I want to talk about that sermon you gave on Sunday," he says. I sit down and endure a thirty-minute lecture on how he disagrees with my interpretation of scripture. It really is OK to me that he doesn't think the way I do about God. What gets me down is his tone. Like a father reprimanding a child, he goes on and on about how I should preach more like his favorite TV preacher. I smile and nod, but inside, my heart breaks.

Finally, he finishes, and I go back upstairs. *Be still*, I remind myself, *and know God is God. I am not God (thank goodness!). I am not going to be perfect no matter how hard I try.*

I work a bit more until again the intercom sounds. "Heather, come downstairs." Yes, yes, now what? Down I go to the basement level to find a giant puddle of water. "I think the water fountain is broken," my assistant says. As there is water all over the floor, I agree with her.

She goes back upstairs to answer the phone, and I go to find a mop. While I work, I think about the sermon I am writing. How can I be more positive as that angry parishioner wants? How can I even have time to write a sermon while I am mopping up water in the basement? Is this what being a pastor is?

My phone rings, and it is my son's school. "Your son, Henry, has a fever. You need to come pick him up." I finish the mopping and head out the door. "I'll be back in a bit," I holler to my assistant.

"I'm leaving early today," she replies.

I pick up my son, get him home, and head back to the office. My assistant is gone, so now I am answering the phone while I try to work on this week's message. "Hello? . . . No, we don't need new insurance." "Hello? . . . No, we can't pay your water bill today." "Hello? . . . No, I don't want to buy your Bible study." "Hello?" "Hello?" "Hello?" No time to actually work, as the day hurriedly rushes on. What about my sermon preparation? *Be still*, I remind myself.

Three o'clock rolls around. I pick up my daughter from school, and when I get home, I get busy again. I gather and sort the mail, I take out the trash, I do a bit of reading for Sunday school preparation, and I make dinner. By 5 p.m., I am out the door again for a meeting at the church. I sure didn't get a chance to "be still" during that break.

At the church's council meeting, we are talking finances—my least favorite subject. We have big dreams, lots of ideas, and not enough money to make it all happen. I do my best to keep everyone civil, but it doesn't take long for fighting to ensue. Everyone wants money for their favorite things—music, youth group, homeless ministry, food bank—but there's not enough money for everything. We end the meeting without a decision, and I am drained from the conflict in the room.

As I drive home, tears begin to fall. I pull into an empty parking lot and look up at the night sky. I pray, *God, what are You doing with me? Why did You call me to be a pastor? I can't do all these things. Between being a parent and being a pastor, there is no time for me. My heart is breaking, Lord. What would You have me do? Please show me a way out of this mess.*

Be still are the words that come into my heart and mind. *Be still, and know that I am God.* I breathe deeply and close my eyes. God is God, and I am not. God will take care of things at church. God will take care of things at home. God will take care of me!

I realize I don't need to do it all; I just need to do my best. God will be exalted no matter what I do. God is so much bigger than my church or my life. God has this.

I dry my eyes and drive home. *Be still, and know*, I tell myself. Know that God has this under control, and I don't have to.

Faith Step
Is there anything you are holding on to too tightly? Is there any part of your life where you are trying too hard? What could you let go of? How could you "be still" and let God be God?

God's Right Hand

TERRIE TODD

"Do not fear், for I am with you; do not be dismayed, for I am your God. I will strengthen you and help you; I will uphold you with my righteous right hand."

—Isaiah 41:10, NIV

In May 1995, a job layoff spurred my husband, Jon, to accept a job with a potato farmer to tide us over until something more permanent came along. He enjoyed the work, the people, and the return to his farming roots. By fall, the harvest crew was putting in grueling hours. Jon's job was driving a semitruck from the potato field to the processing plant, sometimes numerous times each day.

On September 29, our lives changed forever. While Jon was attempting to brush some dirt away from the belt of a live-bottom trailer, his glove became caught between the belt and roller. The powerful rollers, designed to move tons of potatoes, easily pulled his right arm through, trapping him until a coworker came to his aid. Freeing him from the machinery required several men. By the end of the day, Jon found himself settled into a hospital bed, his right arm amputated about five inches above the elbow.

That night I explained to our children—ages fourteen, twelve, and eight—what had happened to their dad. After tucking them in, I crawled into my own bed. Fearful for our future, I turned to my Bible for comfort. I read the precious promise in Isaiah 41:10. Though my husband's right arm was gone, God's arm would hold us fast. I slept well, knowing in whose hands our hope rested.

Our eighteenth wedding anniversary fell two days later. I drifted off to sleep that night with the words of our marriage vows running through my head: "For better, for worse, in sickness and in health, till death do us part." How thankful I felt that death had not parted us yet and that God had equipped Jon for this arduous challenge by giving him a patient, determined, and resourceful spirit. Some might call it stubbornness.

Jon stayed in the hospital for a week and then underwent physiotherapy. Such a loss leaves much to deal with at once. If you can't imagine his new reality, try this: Tie your dominant hand behind your back. Now shower, dress, and insert your contact lenses. Butter your toast, open a milk carton, and peel an orange. Don't forget to take the pain medication they put in a childproof container for you. Tie your boots and zip your coat.

Now drive your standard-transmission car to town. Do your banking (your signature will look different from now on). Visit the post office and the employment office. Wonder what your future holds. Where will you work? How will you provide for your family? Add to this some serious pain in your shoulder area and frequent blasts of electric shock-like pain to the hand behind your back. Try to grasp that tomorrow you need to do it all again. And the day after that. And the day after that . . .

On the upside, imagine dozens of cards arriving for you, fruit baskets, groceries, and meals. Imagine your church family collecting money and helping with farmwork, snowblowing, and winterizing your home. Know that hundreds of prayers are going up for you. Feel their power as God sustains you and gives you grace to thank Him for sparing your life. Know that He has a plan in this, that it did not surprise Him. Observe as others are blessed and drawn closer to God because of it. Enjoy the closeness among family members that comes with facing trials together. Know that you're loved and cared for by more people than you ever realized. Experience in a new way the peace of God, which surpasses all understanding as it guards your heart and mind.

That's all history now.

Someone asked me recently how Jon's disability changed *my* life. Now there's a loaded question. Where do I begin?

A friend who never knew my husband with two arms said, "I never think of Jon as having only one arm." I rarely do either. Jon's arm (or lack thereof) no longer consumes my life as it did in those early days and months. However, I believe I've learned much over the years as I've returned to the promise of God's right hand upholding us.

I've learned that one can question God and survive. What do you do with a faith that knows God can heal but asks why He does not? In my limited experience, every instance of physical healing I've heard of has, without fail, been an internal or invisible ailment—a tumor, arthritic joints, or a headache. People stand and testify to how doctors diagnosed a horrible condition that later disappeared. I've found myself doubtfully thinking, *How do I know a tumor ever existed? How do I know your pain wouldn't have subsided anyway? How do I know the doctors weren't mistaken in their diagnosis? If God caused my husband's arm to grow back, the whole world would notice, wouldn't they? No one could say, "How do I know his arm was ever really gone?"* Although hearing about others' healings no longer angers me, I still don't understand how they work. I do know, however, that God has not struck me dead for such faithless questions.

I think I've learned to show more care and consideration. I'll change the toilet paper roll before it runs out so Jon won't need to. I leave the twist-tie off the bread bag and place his silverware and cup to the left of his plate. I slice his bagels in half and button his shirt. Little things like that.

I've been introduced to a deplorable side of myself, a side that hopes others will view me as some brave saint—which leads to guilt. Then there's the guilt for not cheerfully helping him more with the frustrating challenges of daily life. Guilt for feeling ticked with him over the same grievances that would have ticked me off before the accident. Guilt for feeling cheated out of two-armed hugs. I offer no excuse.

In contrast to the above, I've learned gratitude. I'm grateful for a husband who survived, who can walk and talk and think, who loves me, stays with me, and has done his best to support his family when many able-bodied men do not. I thank God for His faithfulness in meeting our needs.

I've learned to anticipate heaven more. There, we'll enjoy perfect, healthy, beautiful bodies that will never grow weary, minds that will never think selfish or evil thoughts, and souls that will worship God forever. With this knowledge, we look to the future with joy.

Through the tears, anger, and frustration, God made Himself real. He is our Peace, our Hope, our Rock, our Savior.

Faith Step

Because God promises to uphold you with His right hand, you don't need to fear. To which struggle in your life does this most apply? Tell God about it. Commit Isaiah 41:10 to memory and use it to steady you when fear rises.

Small Beginnings

RACHAEL ADAMS

"Who dares despise the day of small things?"

—Zechariah 4:10, NIV

Our dreams don't always happen in the way or time we think they should. Our instant gratification culture expects an immediate outcome to our obedience and effort. We may struggle to continue working toward a goal when we hit a roadblock, when achieving our goal takes longer than expected, or when our work feels mundane and insignificant. In the rhythm of daily tasks and juggling various responsibilities, I sometimes feel as though what I'm doing doesn't matter much in the grand scheme of things. Is my life meaningless?

This isn't a new feeling for me. It's something I've wrestled with for years, ever since I was a freshman in college. At that time, I had big dreams of becoming a broadcast journalist. I signed up for a broadcast journalism class, excited about the possibility of reporting important stories and impacting lives through media. But as the semester went on, something unexpected happened: I realized I wasn't as good at public speaking as I'd hoped. I struggled with nerves, and the pressure of being on camera left me feeling inadequate. The dream I'd carried so confidently began to feel out of reach.

Feeling discouraged, I decided to switch majors, choosing business management instead. As I closed the door on my broadcast journalism dream, I couldn't shake the feeling that I had failed. In my heart, I wondered if I had missed my chance to do something meaningful.

Years passed, and life moved on. I pursued other career paths, became a wife and mother, and embraced new roles. But that feeling of inadequacy and the longing for more always lingered in the background. I would see people on TV or hear stories of others accomplishing great things and feel the sting of comparison. Why didn't my dreams turn out the way I imagined?

Then, one day, something began to shift. Through my church involvement, I started finding new opportunities to connect with people. One Sunday, I was sitting in the church pew and saw a love offering envelope in front of me. Typically, these are for monetary giving; however, I sensed the Lord saying, *Rachael, you are My love offering. I have given you My love. How are you going to give My love to the world around you?* That simple moment was the beginning of *The Love Offering* podcast, where I interview people who share stories of encouragement, faith, and love.

Slowly, over time, I became more comfortable speaking—whether behind the microphone on my podcast or on small stages at local events. Little by little, God built my confidence and equipped me with skills I hadn't fully realized I was developing. Simultaneously, I led Bible study within my church and wrote for various publications. After attending a writers' conference, I met an agent who believed in me and the love offering message God had laid on my heart. After two years of working on my proposal to pitch to publishers, I started writing my first traditionally published book.

After promoting my book on various media outlets, I received an opportunity I never expected—an invitation to be on *Good Morning America*. As I prepared for the interview, I couldn't help but reflect on the journey that had led me there. Nearly two decades after I had abandoned my dream of broadcast journalism, I was about to be on one of the most well-known television shows in the country. The dream I had carried in college had finally come true but in a completely different way than I had imagined. God had been working behind the scenes all along, using the small, everyday moments of faithfulness to prepare me for something greater.

It was then that Zechariah 4:10 came to life for me: "Do not despise these small beginnings, for the LORD rejoices to see the work begin" (NLT). The context of this verse is incredibly powerful. The Jewish people, returning from exile, were tasked with rebuilding the Temple of Jerusalem. They were discouraged because the new temple they were constructing wasn't as grand or beautiful as the original temple built by Solomon. It felt small and insignificant in comparison, and they wondered if their efforts even mattered. But Zechariah, a minor prophet, encouraged them with a message from God. He reminded them that it wasn't the size or beauty of the temple that made it significant but the presence of God within it. God wasn't focused on the outward appearance—He rejoiced in their work, no matter how small it seemed.

This message resonated deeply with me. For so long, I had focused on what I thought my life should look like on the outside—whether it was achieving certain dreams or measuring up to the success I saw in others. But God's perspective is so different from ours. He isn't concerned with how impressive or grand our lives appear from the outside. What matters most to Him is that we are faithful to the work He has given us, however small it may seem.

At that moment, I realized that even during those years where I felt as though I wasn't doing enough, God had been with me all along, rejoicing in the small beginnings. God was in the podcast episodes recorded in my quiet home office, in the local speaking engagements, and in the countless hours of writing and prayer. He had been building something in me that didn't look grand or impressive at first glance but was filled with His presence.

The same is true for you. Maybe you feel as though your life is filled with small tasks that don't seem to matter. Perhaps you're in a season of small beginnings, wondering if your work will ever lead to something bigger. But just as Zechariah encouraged the people of Israel, God is encouraging each of us today. He delights in our small beginnings, and He sees the significance of our work because He is in it.

One of the most profound lessons I've learned is that God doesn't measure success the way we do. He isn't waiting for us to achieve something grand before He blesses us with His approval. Instead, He is with us in the small moments, the everyday acts of faithfulness, and the quiet steps of obedience. He rejoices when we trust Him with the little things, knowing He is working them together for a greater purpose.

Take heart if you're feeling discouraged by the size of your work or the season you're in. God is with you in the small things. He sees your faithfulness and uses every moment to shape you for the future He has planned for you. Don't despise the small beginnings—celebrate them because they are where God is doing some of His most significant work.

When I look back at the journey that led me to *Good Morning America*, I'm reminded of how faithful God has been, even when I couldn't see it. He took a dream I thought was lost and brought it to life in a more beautiful and impactful way than I ever imagined. And He can do the same for you.

Faith Step

Today, pause and reflect on the small tasks or beginnings that may feel insignificant. Ask God to help you see His presence in them and to remind you that He rejoices in your faithfulness, no matter how small it seems. Trust that God is using these moments to prepare you for something greater and celebrate His work, both seen and unseen.

Caregiving

REBECCA D. BRUNER

When Jesus saw his mother there, and the disciple whom he loved standing nearby, he said to her, "Woman, here is your son," and to the disciple, "Here is your mother." From that time on, this disciple took her into his home.

—John 19:26–27, NIV

"How was your day?" my husband asked as we sat down to dinner.

"Exhausting!" I felt emotionally weary and physically spent. This had been a very tough week, and today had been the hardest of all.

I had taken my mother to three different medical appointments on three different days. On Monday, she went to the ophthalmologist to get shots in her eyes to prevent her macular degeneration from advancing any further.

On Tuesday, I took her to the vascular specialist for ultrasounds of her circulatory system. We showed up to the office on time, only to learn that the location where her appointment had been scheduled was over twenty miles away.

Mom's face fell. "I'm really sorry," she said as we climbed back into my car. It was obvious that she felt horrible.

Taking a deep breath, I restarted the engine. "It's OK, Mom," I said. "It was a mistake. These things happen."

Her eyesight is bad enough that she had not recognized a different address in the reminder text she'd received about the appointment. By the grace of God, they were still able to run all her scheduled tests once we arrived, even though we were so late.

Today was Thursday. The morning had been consumed by our weekly shopping trip. We visited several different grocery stores, as usual. Instead of going home after that, we had picked up lunch and then headed back to the vascular specialist's office to get the results of the tests they had run earlier in the week. I had left at 8:30 that morning and had not returned home until after 3:00 that afternoon.

My husband shook his head. "No wonder you're exhausted!"

It would be tempting on such occasions to feel frustrated and resentful. I could easily view my mother's needs as an imposition, getting in the way of the things I'd like to accomplish. But then Jesus reminds me that He is the one who called me to care for her.

I am the only child of a single mother. I took this fact for granted growing up, never having known things any other way. As a young woman, I never stopped to consider what having no siblings would mean for me as Mom aged.

It wasn't until I reached my thirties, when the company my husband worked for planned to relocate to Colorado, that I began to think more seriously about how being an only child might impact my future.

"We can't move," I told my husband. "We really need to stay in Arizona, near my mom. She has no other family." Mom was still working full-time. Our family stayed put, and my husband found a different job.

Years passed. My mom retired. As she got older, her health began to deteriorate.

Eventually, the second-story condominium where she had lived for over twenty years became impractical. Pain in her knees meant that she limited her trips downstairs. She developed macular degeneration and glaucoma. Driving at night became unsafe. Whenever she came to our house for a visit, she had to spend the night so she didn't have to risk driving the twenty-five miles from our place to hers in the dark. At the age of seventy-five, she moved into a single-story condominium just two miles from our home.

Soon after that, getting behind the wheel at all became too dangerous. "I think it's time for me to give up driving," Mom told me. "I had a really close call in the parking lot, and I just don't feel safe."

It was hardly a surprise. I should have been grateful that she'd made the decision on her own instead of my having to confiscate her keys. But somehow, I didn't feel very grateful.

I would be forced to assume more responsibility for getting her places, I knew. Her independence was diminishing, and I was wrestling with how that would impact me.

At church on Palm Sunday that year, the sermon focused on the last sayings of Christ on the cross. The pastor emphasized how difficult it would have been for Jesus to say anything. Crucifixion causes slow suffocation. Every breath is torture. To exhale, Jesus had to push His full body weight upward, fighting against the pull of gravity and the nails that pierced His feet and hands, affixing Him to the cross. Drawing enough breath to speak must have been agonizing.

"If ever there is a time when you can expect a person to think only of himself," the pastor said, "it is at the hour of his death. Yet even in the agony of His final hours on the cross, Jesus thought of others."

The pastor went on to talk about how Christ took notice of His mother, Mary. She stood at the foot of His cross, overcome with grief. A sword was piercing His mother's own soul, just as Simeon had prophesied when Mary brought Jesus to the temple as an infant.

Jesus thought about His mother's future. At that time, His own brothers did not yet believe in Him (John 7:4–5). They might have cared for Mary's physical needs, but they would have given little thought for her spiritual well-being.

Jesus saw John, one of His closest friends. John had been with Him on the Mountain of Transfiguration, had glimpsed that revelation of His glory. John had leaned against Jesus's chest at the Last Supper, the evening prior to His Crucifixion. John had been one of the three whom He had begged to stay awake and pray in the final hours before His arrest.

Struggling against the pain that tore through His limbs, Jesus fought for enough breath to say to Mary, "Woman, here is your son," and then to John, "Here is your mother." John took Mary into his home from that time on.

In the quiet of my heart, I felt Jesus speaking to me, "My mother's care was a top priority for Me. Your mother's care should be very important to you too."

Instead of seeing my mother's decreasing independence as something that would hinder my ability to work and exercise my gifts in ministry, I realized this was a new assignment from Jesus Himself.

Faith Step

The needs of our aging parents are bound to increase over time. Our attitude about them will make all the difference. Do we cherish the opportunity to care for them? Or do we resent the way their needs make demands upon our freedom? When it comes to the needs of our own aging parents, we should joyfully follow Jesus's example, doing as our Lord did.

What's in a Word?

LOIS HUDSON

> But be very careful to obey all the commands and the instructions that Moses gave to you. Love the LORD your God, walk in all his ways, obey his commands, hold firmly to him, and serve him with all your heart and all your soul.
>
> —Joshua 22:5, NLT

In concluding his sermon one Sunday, my pastor said something that jolted me to attention and made me wonder, *Does the Bible really say that?* My question unsettled me and made me realize I didn't know the Bible as well as I thought I did—or should. It's been over forty years since that day, and I couldn't tell you what the pastor said. His words were not the catalyst; it was my question that fueled my spirit's passion to learn more.

I'd like to say I was a truth seeker, but that would not be the truth. I was a social Christian, going to church, getting my infusion of inspiration, and forgetting all about it by Tuesday. But this time, my interest didn't wane. I told my husband I wanted to get into a real Bible study. But there was one problem with that. We had just transferred our membership to a church plant in the suburbs. The new church had not yet established classes or small groups; the only Bible study we were receiving was excellent but came from the weekly sermons. The young pastor recommended that we attend fall classes that a large church of a different but compatible denomination was offering. That appealed to me. The church was less than a mile from our home. I could even walk to it. I read the literature from the class and immediately felt let down. They were going to spend an entire year studying only one book of the Bible. That wouldn't do. I was in a hurry. I wanted to know what the whole Bible said.

When I confided my disappointment to my best friend, she immediately invited me to join a women's class at her church, where the plan was to read through and study the Bible in one year. Obviously that could not be a comprehensive study, but it would give me an overview, a place to start.

I wasn't completely unfamiliar with the Bible's teachings. I was a pastor's kid, after all. I heard my father preach every Sunday, but, as a rather self-absorbed child, I tuned out much of what he said. Still, I was a preacher's kid, so I was tight with God, right? I remember my baptism at the age of four at a family camp for pastors' families. The camp was high on a hill overlooking Lake Taneycomo in the Missouri Ozarks. I still have the sweet, pink dime-store bowl into which a dear friend of my father's dipped his fingers and touched my head three times. In the name of the Father, and of the Son, and of the Holy Spirit.

So, armed with my old Revised Standard Version of the Bible, a huge three-ring notebook, and a fistful of pens and pencils, I rode with my friend to her church and met a teacher I'll never forget and will be forever grateful for. She passed out the study notes for the first week—seven or eight pages' worth. We started in the New Testament. Every morning after my husband left for work, before my two sons even woke up, I sat at the kitchen table with all my paraphernalia spread out and dug in. There was a different reading assignment every day, followed by questions and thought-starters. I loved it. I've always loved filling out forms. This was going to be fun. The teacher even called me her best student because I asked a lot of questions. I learned to search for answers through cross-referencing different passages, and soon I was able to recognize the holes in my own spiritual understanding.

On my birthday, for a silly treat after my regular study, I began searching for verses that corresponded with any of the numbers of my birthday—11, 22, and 33. There were quite a few misfits.

"When Serug was 30 years old, he became the father of Nahor" (Genesis 11:22, NLT) didn't exactly ring any bells for me. But then I came to Joshua 22:5: "But be very careful to obey all the commands and the instructions that Moses gave to you. Love the LORD your God, walk in all his ways, obey his commands, hold firmly to him, and serve him with all your heart and all your soul" (NLT).

Love the Lord your God. The first and greatest commandment. Easy to say, but did I really?

Walk in all His ways. To do that I had to get to know Jesus up close and personally. That determined my study for the next few months and continues to this day.

Obey His commands. Aye, there's the rub. Why is it so difficult? God has promised that His commands are for my benefit and immeasurably better than anything I can imagine.

Hold firmly to Him. Some translations say *cling*, and because I liked the one-word verbs, I chose to remember it as *cling*. That has been a lifesaver through difficult times in my life when I can't see through the dark.

Serve Him with all your heart. *All* my heart? Oh, may it be!

I am not sure when the reality of the value of these words became embedded in my heart and mind and soul, but in recent months I find myself mentally going through them upon waking every morning. Five simple words that are easy to remember using the fingers of one hand. I have found that they are a great checklist for my personal walk of faith. I've seen the subtle changes from casual Christian to devoted disciple, still on the path.

Faith Step
Pray this verse from Joshua 22 when you wake up every day for a week. How does this verse speak to what it looks like to become a devoted disciple of Christ?

Sit Quietly with Me

JANET LAIRD MULLEN

When Job's three friends, Eliphaz the Temanite, Bildad the Shuhite and Zophar the Naamathite, heard about all the troubles that had come upon him, they set out from their homes and met together by agreement to go and sympathize with him and comfort him. When they saw him from a distance, they could hardly recognize him; they began to weep aloud, and they tore their robes and sprinkled dust on their heads. Then they sat on the ground with him for seven days and seven nights. No one said a word to him, because they saw how great his suffering was.

—Job 2:11–13, NIV

As a college English teacher, I am blessed with many meaningful interactions with my students as we share ideas, craft essays together, and study great works of literature. One of my favorite classes to teach is World Literature I, where we survey ancient texts that still speak powerfully. It is exciting to watch eighteen- and nineteen-year-olds discover themselves in works written more than two thousand years ago.

The story of the suffering servant Job is often anthologized because of its enduring relevance. Its writer wanted to dispel a common and long-held belief in the ancient world: suffering was evidence of sin.

In Job's story, the reality is quite the reverse. It is God's joy in Job that sparks the intense testing that strips him of so much that is dear to him—his children, his material wealth, and, ultimately, his own physical and emotional well-being. But neither Job nor his wife nor his friends realize this. His wife urges him to curse God and die, but his friends get it right, at least initially:

> When Job's three friends, Eliphaz the Temanite, Bildad the Shuhite and Zophar the Naamathite, heard about all the troubles that had come upon him, they set out from their homes and met together by agreement to go and sympathize with him and comfort him. When they saw him from a distance, they could hardly recognize him; they began to weep aloud, and they tore their robes and sprinkled dust on their heads. Then they sat on the ground with him for seven days and seven nights. No one said a word to him, because they saw how great his suffering was. (Job 2:11–13, NIV)

When we discuss this story in class, my Gen Z students pause at this passage. They are all too familiar with the judgments others pass against them. They have heard the pat answers and easy solutions that are often offered by well-meaning people.

What they are not familiar with is the humble, compassionate, quiet act of solidarity that Job's friends offer in the opening scenes of this drama. They hear of Job's sorrow. They come immediately. They express their own grief when they see what their friend is facing. Then they sit down in the dust with their friend. And they say *nothing*. What great discipline it must have taken to sit and keep quiet with Job, to experience his loss along with him, to feel the overwhelming discomfort of the pain and the paralyzing confusion of having no answers, no rationale, no reason. And they were willing just to sit there with him. As long as needed. And to say nothing.

I am blessed to have experienced this depth of true friendship in my own life. It came at a time when I felt as if I had lost everything that mattered most to me: when my husband of twenty-eight years told me he wanted a divorce and bought a new house without my knowledge, taking our daughter with him.

My friends could have come to me curious to know what happened, hungry for juicy gossip about who did what and who was in the wrong. They could have sought out the reasons for his leaving just to reassure themselves that their spouses would not do the same. That they were safe.

But they didn't.

They came and sat with me in the ashes and tears of my sorrow. It was a most uncomfortable place; I was certainly not good company. But compelled by compassion and moved by Christ, they came. And I experienced what true friendship is.

I had friends who offered practical help. One helped me set up my house for life on my own. Another generously made herself available to talk anytime I needed her, even when it meant hearing my same complaints and sorrows again. A third created fun outings, reminding me of the importance of being playful, even in the midst of sorrow. There were others who simply texted from time to time to say they loved me and knew I would get through this.

Each of them offered regular support. The most important thing each of them did was to be present with me—just to offer themselves to me. These people reminded me that friendship is among God's greatest gifts. And the gifts of their friendship pointed me to an even greater gift: God's tenacious friendship with me.

Experiencing this level of empathy and true compassion has changed the way I offer myself to those around me who are suffering. I still offer to pray for them, and I do. I still offer practical help—food or assistance—and I follow through.

But I have lived an important truth: what all of us most need is *presence*. God's presence—and the presence of true friends. I can stand or sit as a human proxy for Him, offering my physical presence and my silence to those I call friend. I can listen to them or simply be there with them in their pain. That is the challenge I now place on my life. That is the kind of friend I now aspire to be.

Faith Step

Who in your life is going through a hard time? Ask the Lord to show you who needs you right now. You can offer yourself in a powerful way to those around you who are suffering. You can and should pray for them. And you can provide whatever practical help that you are able to give—cooking meals, helping out with children or elderly parents, doing yard work, moving furniture. But what your friends most need is you. Commit to a time to go and just be with that person—unhurried, fully attentive. This is not a time to offer advice but simply your humble, compassionate presence.

Even If

SYLVIA SCHROEDER

Shadrach, Meshach and Abed-nego replied to the king, "O Nebuchadnezzar, we do not need to give you an answer concerning this matter. If it be so, our God whom we serve is able to deliver us from the furnace of blazing fire; and He will deliver us out of your hand, O king. But even if He does not, let it be known to you, O king, that we are not going to serve your gods or worship the golden image that you have set up."

—Daniel 3:16–18, NASB1995

"I gave up my daughter today," I wrote in my journal.

Oh, I certainly had given Charity up many times before.

Once as a tiny bundle held in my arms, wrapped in a white gauzy blanket. I shushed her in front of the congregation while she protested with loud cries, and I gave her up to God.

Again, I gave her to God as a rambunctious child full of terrible-two energy and later with prayerful angst in those troublesome teen years.

Then came a day, when she was dressed in a flowing white gown and pearl-studded veil, my husband and I gave her into the care of a young man to love and cherish.

Yet, for all of us who loved Charity, the giving had never held such pain or terror as it did that April, when a brain-stem lesion took away her abilities before our eyes.

"There is no hope," the neurosurgeon said.

Everyone fell silent. Charity and her husband, Jeremy, sat together against the metal hospital headboard, her hand hidden in his.

The words dropped like glass into the silent hospital room. They shattered about our feet, fragile, broken, and still.

And so began a two-year teeter-totter between life and death for our twenty-six-year-old daughter with a young husband, a two-year-old, and a six-month-old baby.

The body of Christ, like an army, moved into position. It lifted, helped, and supported. Yet, each day, in one hospital bed after another, she faded away underneath white sheets and a web of tubes. She could no longer hold her baby and became a stranger to her two-year-old.

Declared first to be an inoperable cancer, the mass became a mystery for the entire team of doctors. No one could definitively diagnose it. It was a nemesis, a monster, and it was killing my daughter.

Running batteries of tests, fleets of specialists scoured for answers, while her mobilities fell like Jenga pieces. The ability to stand, gone. The ability to walk, talk, and think all vanished. The ability to be Charity, lost.

I grieved for the mommy who loved her babies but could not hug or talk to them. She drifted further and further into a foggy world where no one could reach her.

Advice and suggestions poured in along with flowers and cards. People visited and left undone. Nurses huddled in the hallway and cried.

I pled for a miracle, but every day came more of the opposite.

Until early one morning, I stumbled to her side after spending an uncomfortable night on the cot beside her. I'd dreamt that Jesus healed her. It felt so very real, but when I bent down to look into her eyes, they were wide blue orbs of fear.

Doctors had warned that she was heading into a locked-in state. It would leave her unable to move at all, except for her eyes. That dawn, as I laid my head against her forehead, I knew it had happened. She could move nothing at all, except those expressive eyes.

And, in our pleading before God, I agonized, "What, Lord, is there left to give? You have taken it all."

It seemed that the doctor had been right. There was no hope.

Months passed. While she lay in that vegetative state, unresponsive and unreachable, I received a card from a friend. Inside she highlighted verses from the book of Daniel. Those words became an anchor in my storm then and remain a continuing reminder of truth today. "Our God whom we serve is able to deliver us from the furnace of blazing fire; and He will deliver us out of your hand, O king. But *even if* He does not, let it be known to you, O king, that we are not going to serve your gods or worship the golden image that you have set up" (Daniel 3:17–18, NASB1995, emphasis mine).

Three young war captives, Shadrach, Meshach, and Abed-nego, far from home, family, and country, were taken to a pagan land. The king commanded them to bow before his golden image or be thrown into a fiery furnace.

"I've been thinking about these words," my friend wrote in her slanted cursive. "*But even if He does not.* I've been thinking of Charity."

The three young men in the book of Daniel believed God could spare them but also realized they had no guarantee He would. Yet they trusted He knew best.

Our Father's good and perfect will often looks different from ours. Can we trust Him "even if"? The answer is a declared yes.

I gave up Charity anew with this faith step. I scribbled in my journal, "There will be life after this crisis. *Even if.* These are the things I want to be true in my life."

So began my "Even If" list. It started small, but its significance was enormous.

I want to be grateful, not bitter.

I want to trust God more, not less.

I want to worship Him regardless.

As I read and reread the verses my friend gave me, my list grew. The despair I felt began to take new shape.

The story of Shadrach, Meshach, and Abed-nego does not end with a fire. A marvelous thing happened when King Nebuchadnezzar peered into the blaze: there was a fourth man walking in the flames (Daniel 3:23–25).

Shadrach, Meshach, and Abed-nego...

How that comforts me today.

Through my fiery furnace, I discovered that I did not walk alone. Jesus was with me. And though the fire raged around me, I would not be consumed by it. My trajectory of pain changed to one of hope regardless of outcome.

Whatever the circumstance—even if I don't get the job, even if I'm maligned, even if world events bring chaos, even if a relationship sours—He is able to deliver. But even if He does not, He will accomplish great things. I declare God already the victor, however He chooses to respond.

Shadrach, Meshach, and Abed-nego came out of that furnace alive. Their hair wasn't singed, their clothes weren't burnt, nor did the smell of smoke linger on them. God allowed them to go through the fire with Him by their side.

Today Charity and Jeremy live within the constraints of the countless disabilities of incomplete quadriplegia, yet I am grateful our daughter is alive and back. We would have chosen a different ending, but with a smile she says, "I love my life." Her husband has loved her through sickness and health. She is now mom to three vibrant and happy girls. The joy of Jesus is so very evident in their home. They are not alone.

When I need reminding, I read again the verses my friend wrote on that card. I remember He is able. He will do what is best and right. There is purpose in the fire. I am not alone.

Faith Step

Consider times when you prayed for something that didn't come to pass. Write Daniel 3:17–18 on a piece of paper. Let it remind you that God is sovereign in every *even if*.

Think about Such Things

CHANTEL MATHSON

Whatever is true, whatever is noble, whatever is right, whatever is pure, whatever is lovely, whatever is admirable—if anything is excellent or praiseworthy—think about such things.

—Philippians 4:8, NIV

The night had been long, and worry, fear, and exhaustion clung to me like a thick blanket I couldn't shake off. The night before, I had received upsetting news that there had been a helicopter crash within my husband's unit. As a military spouse, those notifications are our worst nightmare, and we often find ourselves waiting for news we hope will never come.

I had spent hours waiting for updates, my mind racing through every possible scenario. Would my husband be OK? Would someone in our close-knit community lose a loved one? Fear twisted my thoughts into a knot, and I found myself going down a path of what-ifs, imagining the heartbreak that could unfold. In the middle of this struggle, my sweet infant daughter called out for me, her voice soft but insistent. It was enough to break the hold of my spiraling thoughts, at least for a moment.

Her cry pulled me back to reality as I knew she needed me, here and now. I scooped her up, holding her close, and I tried to release the worry. While my mind had been consumed with fear and anxiety, she had been waiting, unaware of the storm swirling in my head. She didn't know what was happening, and I worried her innocent heart could one day be shattered by news like this, but right now, she was blissfully free from those worries.

In that moment, I realized I had a choice. I could continue to let my mind be consumed by the unknown, dwelling on fears that may or may not come true, or I could turn my focus to something more positive. I could choose to focus on what I knew to be true—the solid foundation of God's Word and His promises—and to seek His peace in the midst of uncertainty.

Philippians 4:8 is a verse that has anchored me many times in the past, and it came to mind as I tried to change my focus: "Whatever is true, whatever is noble, whatever is right, whatever is pure, whatever is lovely, whatever is admirable—if anything is excellent or praiseworthy—think about such things."

I wanted to hold on to this truth as I navigated my worries. My anxious thoughts were pulling me into a pit, but this verse reminded me that I didn't have to live there. Instead of dwelling on what might happen, I could focus on what is true. I could focus on what is lovely like the warmth of my daughter in my arms, her innocence, or the sound of her breath as she rested.

As I held her and we rocked together in the dim light of her nursery, I pulled out my Bible, seeking comfort. I began to pray, reciting Philippians 4:8 aloud, allowing its words to fill the anxious spaces in my heart. "Whatever is true . . . whatever is lovely . . ." I repeated the verse, asking God to help me turn my thoughts toward these things. My heart was still heavy with the uncertainty of what might come, but I began to feel a shift. The fear that had gripped me began to loosen, just a little, as I turned my focus from the unknown to the truth of who God is.

What is true? Focusing on what is true in moments of fear and anxiety can be incredibly difficult. Our minds tend to fixate on worst-case scenarios, imagining the things that could go wrong. But Paul implores us to consider the truth of our situation—and, more important, the truth about God in this situation. The truth is that God is with us, even when our circumstances feel overwhelming and aren't what we hoped for or expected. His presence brings peace, even when we don't have all the answers and chaos surrounds us. He is sovereign, even when life feels out of control.

In my moment of anxiety, I didn't know if the worst possible news would be coming. I had reason to worry, but shifting my focus to God's promises calmed my heart as I waited. Focusing on the goodness of God reminded me that He was with me and would be through it all. That night was spent focusing on God's faithfulness and the sweetness of my little girl instead of thinking about what might come. Each time my mind would wander, I would recite Philippians 4:8 and remind myself that God is faithful, He is present, and He offers peace. Focusing on what is true doesn't mean ignoring our problems or pretending everything is fine. We still acknowledge the reality of our circumstances while anchoring ourselves in the unchanging truth of God's character and holding on to His peace.

What is lovely? In times of fear and uncertainty, it's easy to become fixated on the harshness of our circumstances. But even in the hardest moments, there is beauty to be found. For me, the loveliness was in the warmth of my daughter's embrace, her trust, and the sweetness of being her mom. But beyond that, I was reminded of the way God weaves moments of grace and beauty into even the darkest days. His presence alone should give us comfort as we navigate difficulties. Keeping focus on God allows us to settle into whatever is to come and embrace the discomfort of the unknown. Clinging to the lovely helps us walk through the struggles with more peace.

Shifting our focus onto what is lovely reminds us of the beauty God has placed in our lives, even when things feel chaotic. It might be a kind word, a moment of laughter, or the stillness of nature. When we actively seek out the lovely, we change our perspective, and peace follows.

As I continued to pray and focus on the words of Philippians 4:8, my daughter and I finally drifted off to sleep, resting not because the situation had changed but because my perspective had. In the midst of the uncertainty, God's peace had settled over me like a comforting blanket. It wasn't the absence of problems but the presence of God that brought me peace. God can bring us peace if we focus on Him instead of our troubles and circumstances.

Faith Step

The next time fear or anxiety overwhelms, take a moment to reflect on Philippians 4:8. Start by acknowledging your feelings, but instead of allowing your mind to dwell on what might happen, make a conscious choice to focus on what is true about your situation and God. Then look for the lovely. Is there a moment of beauty, grace, or joy that you can focus on, even if everything else feels hard? Finally, invite God into the moment. Pray and ask for Him to guard your heart and mind. Trust that He is with you, offering peace as you choose to fix your heart on what is true and lovely.

God Is My Refuge

YVETTE BABS WALKER

Whoever dwells in the shelter of the Most High will rest in the shadow of the Almighty. I will say of the LORD, "He is my refuge and my fortress, my God, in whom I trust."

—Psalm 91:1–2, NIV

I turned the key in the lock and opened the front door with unease.

It had been years since my failed marriage, but this simple act could cause flashbacks: coming home from work to find my house wrecked and husband asleep. Dan was unable to do much else. He could easily sleep twelve to sixteen hours a day.

Back then, I had a house, but I really wanted a home. Back then, I was married to a man I couldn't fix and a relationship I didn't understand. Home wasn't a refuge. I believed in the Lord, but I did not know how to find refuge in Him.

God, was that really Your plan for me?

Dan suffered from depressive bipolar disorder and, with it, the constant fatigue and occasional manic episodes. We were married for thirteen years. He had trouble keeping a job. Home all day, he caused messes from room to room for me to clean up after my full day of work. He was too tired to go out with friends. The quiet house was like a tomb.

I didn't expect that life.

But ten years later, after the divorce, I found myself lost. I desperately wanted to be in a loving relationship, but I struggled to find one. And even my former husband was gone. He died a few years after our divorce when a heart attack took his life. I felt like a widow, but I could not claim that title.

And even though I knew my beautiful house was just as I left it, coming home and turning the key in the lock brought up echoes of pain. The emotional toll and guilt of navigating Dan's illness, then failing to make the marriage work, and, finally, not finding my next love, left me drained and questioning my worth.

It wasn't always this way.

Dan and I married in a Catholic church in Dallas. We were in love. He was cute, kind, and we shared lots of interests—movies, books, his saxophone. We couldn't wait to start our lives together.

I loved his big brain—his knowledge of film, history, and music—as much as his kindness to animals. When we first met at a French pastry shop, I forgave his drowsy eyes and constant yawns. He said it wasn't me. I believed him; I just figured it was work. In the beginning, I ignored his always messy apartment (he was a bachelor, right?), and I even forgave the fact that he didn't go to church regularly. That would change, I figured.

But a year into the marriage, one night I could take it no longer and blew up about his lack of cleanliness around the house. He told me the new diagnosis that would change the rest of our lives: bipolar disorder.

I looked up symptoms to understand what he was facing. I saw crippling fatigue, sure, but there were more: feeling sad, hopeless or worthless; lacking energy; loss of interest in activities you once enjoyed; difficulty concentrating; thoughts of death or suicide.

That last one threw me. And, for a while, I feared that turning the key in the lock could mean more than a messy house. What would I find when I got home? Would I find him dead?

An old friend told me something that surprised me—that I sounded depressed. Well, isn't that something? I guess I was, in my own way.

With the bipolar disorder came the occasional bout of mania, and Dan would do a 180-degree change. He'd be up several nights without sleep, researching ideas for plans that would never materialize.

Let me be clear, he was sick, and this was not his fault. I didn't blame him. You know who else I didn't blame? God. But I sure wondered where He was and what He was doing in all this.

When I discovered the encouraging words of Psalm 91 years later, I knew that I had missed the opportunity to cling to God in this time of trial. I missed knowing that He was the refuge I desired.

When I filed for divorce three years later, I blamed myself. I had rejected my vows and my promises. But I was determined to find a new partner—someone who could feel like the home and refuge that I so desperately wanted. So I threw myself back into dating and trying to find my next love but with no success.

A few years after the divorce and several boyfriends, I had what I call a "long night of the soul." I couldn't sleep. I lay in bed crying, unable to find any peace. By then, I was getting to be what some people call "a woman of a certain age," and I was afraid I'd be alone for the rest of my life.

And then . . .

Christian radio was playing on the bedside nightstand, and a song came on. I never put much stock into the idea that God could send a song to comfort me at just the right time until that moment. The song was "More" by Matthew West.

West sings from the viewpoint of God, and He tells us, His people, how He created everything—the stars, the moon, the sun—and even though He did all that, He loves us more.

Right then, right there, a switch turned on. God (through Matthew West) helped me realize something for the first time. It wasn't that I was afraid of being alone. I was afraid I'd never be loved again.

And you know what? I didn't need that fear because God loves me, now and forever. So what did I have to be afraid of? Nothing!

God told me my current focus would yield nothing holy and that I should spend some time with Him instead. So I did.

How long would God take me off the dating market? He didn't tell me up front, so I had to go on faith. And when I look back, I really don't remember much of those eighteen months. But I do remember when God said it was OK to return.

I had changed by then. What I was looking for had changed too. This time, I sought a man with a real relationship with Jesus—not someone who went to church occasionally, not someone who didn't pray.

I was different, and I was looking for something different. About six months after I started dating again, I found my future husband. We look forward to celebrating our eighth wedding anniversary in 2025. And when I read Psalm 91, I feel the shelter. I feel the refuge.

I never expected to have a life full of such lessons learned.

Now, when I come home, I'm no longer afraid of what to find when I enter. I know my dwelling is protected by my Lord and Savior. My new key opens a lock that is greater than any door. This key provides the solution to finding joy and happiness.

I know God will keep me safe from harm as long as I remember that He loved me first.

Faith Step

When you are feeling fear in your present situation, read Psalm 91 and draw a simple picture of a house—roof, walls, front door. On each side of the house, use words to describe all the ways God protects you and offers refuge from your fears.

God the Singer

ALLISON LYNN FLEMMING

"The LORD your God is with you, the Mighty Warrior who saves. He will take great delight in you; in his love he will no longer rebuke you, but will rejoice over you with singing."

—Zephaniah 3:17, NIV

One of my favorite childhood memories is standing with my mom in the church pew. As the organ started to play its opening chords, I tucked myself under her arm and leaned in close. We shared her hymnal. I heard our voices weave together. All around us, our church family joined in the song.

Those early memories of voices lifted in praise became the foundation of my life. As soon as I was old enough, I joined one choir and then another. With lots of encouragement, I started to sing solos. Music filled every moment of my life. Soon, my path became clear. I wasn't just someone who loved to sing—I was a singer.

I began the first steps of my career performing recitals, fronting a big band, and performing in musicals. After a few years, God put the final piece in place—I wasn't just called to sing; I was called to sing the gospel.

My fiancé, Gerald, was incredibly supportive. As a professional songwriter and performer himself, he knew the power of this newfound calling. One afternoon he said, "If you're serious about Christian music, we should move to Nashville."

Less than a year after our wedding, we were transplanted and living in Nashville, aka Music City! Within a few months, we'd recorded my first album. It was a tremendous experience, creatively and spiritually. With this accomplishment under my belt, we took the next brave step—we entered the Christian music industry.

We attended festivals and industry events to showcase my songs and rub shoulders with the best in the biz. Our weekends were packed with late-night dinners, inside jokes, and promises of "Let's work together!" It was heady, exciting, and fulfilling.

But get too close to something shiny, and you start to see its imperfections.

I came to Christian music as a fan. Call me naive, but I imagined the artists to be paragons of virtue, lives perfectly aligned with the messages they sang. And, honestly, most people were exactly what they claimed to be—genuine, gracious, humble disciples of Christ. But not everyone fit that description.

More times than I want to admit, I witnessed "good Christians" preaching one life in public and living another behind the scenes. I met artists who valued financial wealth, radio success, and awards above ministry. I heard tales of infidelity, emotionally distant parents, and broken relationships.

It was one thing to realize my musical idols were simply flawed humans. In many ways, it was a relief! It meant there was space for my own imperfections. But I couldn't reconcile the hypocrisy. How could these people preach the Gospel when they lived with so many lies? Did I really want to be part of an industry that seemed to reward such duplicity?

In the midst of this struggle, I attended a large music gathering. Late in the evening, a group I didn't know entered the stage. The lead singer stepped forward and said, "God is a singer. Did you know that?"

Wait! What did he just say?

I knew God loved music, had a voice, and could speak. But had I ever pictured God as a singer? The artist quoted Zephaniah 3:17: "The LORD your God is with you, the Mighty Warrior who saves. He will take great delight in you; in his love he will no longer rebuke you, but will rejoice over you with singing" (NIV).

I couldn't believe I'd never noticed that verse before!

The rest of the night was a blur. Those words kept running through my mind—God "will rejoice over you with singing!" God is a singer! Over the next weeks, I started to dig through my Bible. I had only one question—how do we know that God sings?

Job 38:7 says that while God created the world, "the morning stars sang together" (NIV). There was music right from the beginning! I was reminded of the creation of Narnia in C. S. Lewis's *The Magician's Nephew*, where Aslan, Lewis's figure for God, sings Narnia into existence. What a beautiful image of God birthing a world of song from a song!

In the Gospels, we hear God's singing voice through Jesus. At the end of the Passover meal, Jesus and his friends sing a hymn (Matthew 26:30). The next day, Jesus cries out from the cross, "My God, my God, why have you forsaken me?" We usually speak these words from Psalm 22, but the tradition in Jesus's time was to sing the psalms. Some scholars believe that Jesus actually may have sung these words from the cross, just as we might cry out "How Great Thou Art" or "Amazing Grace" in our time of need.

As I worked my way through this journey, my whole relationship with Christian music and the people who performed it was transformed. I realized that it wasn't my song. I could sing it, maybe even write it, but it was never "my" song. All songs belonged to God! He was the original voice—the creator of keys, rhythm, intervals, and dynamics. Every note, every tone, was first sung on the breath of the Great Musician.

And all the artists I'd met, the seemingly perfect and the obviously flawed, also belonged to God. He'd called each of us to sing His song, knowing that our broken offering would reveal a higher grace and glory.

This gave me such freedom—not only in my singing but also in the way I approached the music industry. If it wasn't my song to own and control, then maybe the industry didn't have to own and control me either.

By this point, Gerald and I were ministering together. With this renewed sense of calling, we created our own ideals for our musical life. Prayer and worship would be the center of everything. Our marriage and family would be more important than any concert. Our songs would be steeped in scripture, and, for that to happen, we had to be steeped in scripture first.

As I write this, our duo Infinitely More (inspired by Ephesians 3:20) is celebrating fifteen years of full-time music ministry. In that time, we've become the artists on stage, recording albums, releasing songs, and, yes, sometimes winning awards. And every day, we pray that the life we preach aligns with the life we lead behind the scenes.

We're not perfect. We fall short of our ideals. Our own shiny finish has been marred by more than a few scratches. But at the end of the day, we know it's not about us. We don't make "our" music on our own. Instead, we are singing along with the Great Singer.

God has invited each of us to join in His eternal song. He was singing it before this world began, and He'll be singing it long after it ends. It's a melody filled with notes of mercy and grace, and there is space for every voice in the choir.

So listen for the song of God! It's all around us. Then lift your voice and join in the singing! As the Psalmist reminds us, "Let everything that has breath praise the LORD" (Psalm 150:6, NIV).

Faith Step

What does it feel like to know that God is singing over you right now? Take a moment to be still and listen. Start humming and singing along with God the Singer.

Home Sweet Home

TINA SAVANT GIBSON

"Do not let your hearts be troubled. You believe in God; believe also in me. My Father's house has many rooms; if that were not so, would I have told you that I am going there to prepare a place for you? And if I go and prepare a place for you, I will come back and take you to be with me that you also may be where I am."

—John 14:1–3, NIV

When the Air Force transferred our family from Illinois to Ohio when I was eleven, the sweet people in our church gave us lots of hugs and one simple wooden plaque inscribed with the words of John 14:1–3.

At the time, I never gave that plaque (or those words) a second thought. I was too wrapped up in the angst of moving away from all my sixth-grade friends. But, for my quiet and very private Mama, that gift was a precious treasure. Whether we lived in base housing for a few months or in a rental home for a few years, it was always one of the first things she unpacked. She hung it by the front door, a spiritual symbol of solace for anyone who came through. Sometimes, I would see her just staring at it, peacefully content, as if she knew something the rest of us didn't. In retrospect, I realize that her display of that plaque was a public expression of her personal faith. Its place of prominence on her wall invited Jesus's comforting words to ignite a conversation or encourage a heart of anyone who visited her home. What a wise woman she was.

When I was in my twenties, Daddy died and Mama moved for the last time to a little white house on a hill, her last residence this side of Heaven. One day, as I helped her unpack, she walked toward the front door with that same old plaque in her hands. I had an idea of what was coming. She glanced over at me as she held it against the wall, eyes glistening, and asked, "What do you think of putting it here?"

Ignoring the deep connection she had with those verses, I replied, "Mama, don't you want to put something else up there, something newer or different—you know, to jazz things up?"

She just smiled and replied in her soft-spoken tone, "Daughter, I think it will look wonderful hanging right here." I wasn't surprised by her response and chalked it up to her dislike of change. I had no idea that thirty years later, I would discover her decision to display it there was truly divine.

A few years ago, Mama was diagnosed with stage 4 colon cancer during a routine physical, and the news shook us both to the core. When it became apparent that death was near, she didn't share her innermost thoughts. I respected her silence, knowing that both of us were dealing with her diagnosis in our own ways. However, little by little, day by day, I witnessed her devastated demeanor transform from disbelief to acceptance, from things seen to things unseen. I wish I could say the same thing happened with me. Instead, I pleaded with God for a miracle instead of accepting that His will be done.

As Mama's decline continued, she relocated to a hospice facility. My husband and I stayed with her around the clock. It wasn't long before she shifted from conversations to unconsciousness. One afternoon, the nurses told us that there hadn't been changes in a while, so we might want to get some real rest back at Mama's house, rather than in the chairs we slept in beside her bed. We were hesitant, but eventually we agreed to leave for just an hour, assured they would call us if we needed to return sooner.

I dreaded the walk through her front door and the realization of never hearing her voice again. Once inside, I heard a holy whisper in my heart: *Do not let your hearts be troubled.* A few minutes later, I felt an overwhelming nudge to head back to the hospice facility. My husband offered to drive me back, but I convinced him to stay there and get some much-needed rest. I told him my feeling was probably nothing and I'd be back soon; then we'd both return later together.

When I walked back into her room, Mama was sleeping on her side. I grabbed her Bible by the bed and said, "Mama, let's see what God has to say to us today." I didn't have a scripture in mind; instead, I closed my eyes and opened it randomly—to John 14. My gasp was audible, and I knew this wasn't a coincidence. Those verses, which comforted Mama's heart and hung by her front door for as long as I could remember, had finally come full circle. After I finished reading them, I laid down beside her and held her close until she relocated to her heavenly home, just a few breaths later. Then I drove back to her little white house on the hill and witnessed the most glorious sunset breaking through the clouds that had been raining all day. Oh, how He loves us.

In the weeks and months that followed Mama's death, while I was cleaning out her house room by room, memory by memory, Jesus's words on her wall held my hand like a best friend. Some days, it was easy to celebrate that Mama was finally and fully alive in the home God promised and prepared for her, the one she so often dreamed about. Yet, on other days, the missing set in so deeply that I refused even to glance at them. Still, God's constant presence was palpable, and His peace was always near.

When that final moving day arrived and the U-Haul truck was all packed, I saved the honor of removing that plaque from the wall for last. As I slowly pulled it off, its worn-out frame suddenly split apart, leaving only the piece with those verses on it in my hands. I paused and took it all in. I pondered the journey of that little wooden plaque and the perfect promises it proclaimed—promises that I didn't understand . . . until I did. Promises that brought Mama joyful anticipation of a home way more enduring than anything here on earth. Promises that consoled her only child with healing and hope after her death and to this day. Promises that remind us, especially in our tender seasons, that we are always seen and so very loved by our Heavenly Father. Promises, home sweet promises, that will never ever die.

Faith Step

Does your family have a touchstone of faith like my mother's plaque? If so, place it in a prominent place in your home. If not, consider what would represent God's abiding faithfulness for you and your family and share this object with them.

Hope and a Future

AMANDA PENNOCK

"For I know the plans I have for you," declares the Lord, "plans to prosper you and not to harm you, plans to give you hope and a future."

—Jeremiah 29:11, NIV

There was a time in my life when I did not feel as though I had any purpose. I have struggled most of my life with addictions, depression, and an anxiety disorder and even attempted suicide at the age of fourteen. I spent years seeing psychologists and therapists. In my childhood home, the word *love* was never spoken. My father was an abusive alcoholic. I started taking drugs and drinking just to escape. It wasn't until I reached rock bottom at the age of fifty-six that I found healing.

On July 4, 2015, I took my last drink. I had been drinking all day before driving. My friend warned that I was going to kill myself or someone else. I hated the person I had become and couldn't even look myself in the mirror. That day, I found myself lying on the floor of my closet crying out to God for help. I had finally reached my bottom and wanted to change, but how?

When I shared with my counselor what had happened over the holiday, she suggested that I find an AA meeting. I had never been to a meeting and really didn't know anything about them. Looking on my phone for meetings in my area, I found one for newcomers, so I decided to go check it out. Thankfully, the only requirement for membership is a desire to stop drinking. I was desperate to get help. After hearing people sharing their stories, I realized that I was an alcoholic and was in the right place.

I was advised to find a mentor to take me through the 12-step program, so I asked an older woman who had been part of the program for many years for help. We met every week and went over one step at a time. She told me that the people there would love me until I could love myself. She taught me that I was special and that God loved me and had a plan for me. Each step that I went through brought me closer to God. The steps helped me to look at myself and ask God to help me to forgive myself and others. I started healing from the inside out. I was encouraged to help others.

I met my future husband at these AA meetings. He had been part of this program for most of his life. He believed in God and was very involved in helping others. I was attracted to his honesty when he shared his stories at the meetings. Even though we were drawn to each other, I knew that getting involved in a relationship was discouraged until you had at least one year of sobriety. A few months after my two-year anniversary of sobriety, we started dating.

I found out that he was interested in gem mining. He asked if I would be open to going mining with him in the Georgia mountains. I didn't even know that there were places to go and do that, but, liking adventure and the mountains, I said yes. The first mine that we went to offered five-gallon buckets of dirt and gems to purchase. There was an area outside that provided a place to use a small shovel to scoop out dirt into a screened box. You then lowered the box under water to see what you had after the dirt washed off. I will never forget those beautiful, sparkling gems that appeared—I was hooked! When we got back home, I started looking up YouTube videos about mining, wanting to learn everything I could.

I discovered that there are diamond and crystal mines located in Arkansas. This is a different type of mining. We purchased shovels, gloves, and five-gallon buckets to put our findings in.

These stones were found naturally in the dusty fields. I can't describe how I felt the first time I found a crystal. It was mostly covered in dirt, and I almost walked right past it. As I got closer, I could see the faint sparkle as the sun hit the tip of the crystal. My husband and I started going to the crystal mines twice a year.

One day I was watching a YouTube video about a TV show called *Turquoise Fever*, which was about a family in Nevada that owned turquoise mines. I learned that they are open to the public for mining tours. We had already collected so many crystals that I had practically filled our yard with them, but I wanted a new adventure. Next stop, Tonopah, Nevada. Living in Texas, we packed up the truck and headed west on the twenty-five-hour drive. Once there, I found enough material to fill a five-gallon bucket.

Mining has become a big part of our lives. We are both retired and love our new hobby. The only problem was that I had way too many rocks, so I had to figure out what to do with them all. Praying about it, I got the idea to start making jewelry to give to others. My husband bought equipment, and I began cutting and shaping the stones. I started making rings, necklaces, bracelets, and keychains. I ordered some gift bags and cards. I would put the piece that I made into the bag, along with a tag explaining what the stone was and which mine it came from. On the back of the tag, I put the scripture Jeremiah 29:11.

I think about so many hurting people in the world who need encouragement and hope. I think about a teenage girl going into a rest area and finding this piece of jewelry and feeling special, then reading the scripture that God has a plan for her to give her hope and a future. I started leaving the gifts on all our trips, including on cruises and at airports. I leave them as part of the tips at restaurants and hotels. I pray and ask God to bring the right person to each gift.

What started as a fun hobby has now become my ministry. Jesus has called us to spread the good news to the world, and He has equipped me to be able to do that. Once I was lost and without hope. I didn't think I had any purpose in life. God has restored me, healed me, and has given me hope and a future, and I've made it my mission to share this with others.

Faith Step

Designate a piece of jewelry or something you wear often (a ring or wedding band, a watch, a bracelet) as your reminder that God has given you hope and a future. Whenever you put it on, remind yourself that God is faithful in His Word.

Hemmed In

JANET LAIRD MULLEN

You hem me in behind and before, and you lay your hand upon me.

—Psalm 139:5, NIV

Returning home from a two-day work trip, I could see furniture had been moved out of the house. My heart plummeted, and I felt sick to my stomach. For weeks, my husband would not answer direct questions about his timeline for moving into the house he had bought for himself, nor would my daughter tell me what she planned to do. But today it was evident. My husband and my daughter were at the house, but all their things and all our pets—save our elderly dog, Emma—were gone.

My daughter approached me with a bouquet of flowers. I had celebrated my fiftieth birthday all alone two days earlier while away at the mandatory statewide curriculum and realignment conference. It had been a strange way to usher in such an important milestone in my life. I accepted the flowers from her—they were beautiful—and I thanked her. She walked away.

Trying to cope with the multitude of feelings surging in my heart at that moment, I retreated to the bedroom my husband and I used to share, now bare of any trace of him. I shut the door, climbed onto the bed, and tried to get ahold of myself. Tears threatened.

This is no good, I told myself. I didn't want my husband or my daughter to see me like this. I felt so extremely vulnerable, and I didn't know what to do about it.

Just then I heard a knock at the bedroom door, and before I could get there, my husband said through the door, "We are leaving."

The finality of his words shook me, emotionally and physically.

I swung the door open to see his back as he retreated down the hallway and joined my daughter in the living room where she was waiting for him. I went to her and embraced her and simply told her, "I love you." She did not respond but only turned and followed her father to the garage. I could hear the engine of the car start, and then it pulled away.

I walked back to the bedroom. I sat back down on the bed. Leaning against the headboard, I pulled my knees to my chest, and I just let the sorrow erupt. I heard strange sounds croaking out of me, sounds that I had never heard before. I gulped and tried to catch my breath. My chest pounded in waves of pain. Then the nausea came full force, and I rushed to the bathroom.

When I returned to the bed, I faced a darkness I had never seen before. The November sun was setting outside, and the house was progressively growing darker. But the pain in my heart and my mind and my soul was much, much blacker. I had no idea what to do.

I felt helpless. I felt hopeless. I felt all alone.

This was the moment of my deepest pain, a pain that had progressively deepened for months as I had faced increasing disappointment and betrayal.

But then something remarkable happened. Something I did not expect.

Fourteen words began repeating in my head. They were words I had committed to memory a year before when my friends Liz and Pooh and Khristi had challenged me to memorize Psalm 139 along with them.

You hem me in behind and before, and you lay your hand upon me.

You hem me in behind and before, and you lay your hand upon me.

You hem me in behind and before, and you lay your hand upon me.

A voice within me kept repeating those words of truth, peace, and comfort. The darkness did not abate, but a powerful spiritual light penetrated my inner darkness.

God stood in that room with me. I felt His hand on my shoulder as He reassured me, "Child, everything is going to be all right. I will see to it."

He stood behind me, and I felt Him shielding me from my painful past. And I could see Him standing in front of me in the hours and days and weeks ahead, giving me His strength to face what felt just moments before like an uncertain and unhappy future. Now it was flooded with His light and His presence. Everything had changed.

On that night and into the days and weeks that followed, I found that God honors our trust in Him in our darkest hours, when we cling to a faith that is stripped bare. I had nothing material or relational to hold on to that night; I did not even have anything left of myself to cling to. Nothing could see me through that deepest despair, nothing but my sheer dependence on Him.

I felt abandoned by my family, but these ancient words from another believer gave me the courage to trust Him and to commit to make it through that night. And the next day. And the day after that.

It is now two years later. The divorce is final. My daughter still lives with her father. She has started college and is working.

Today my ex-husband called me to tell me our daughter had been in a car accident this afternoon when she was merging onto the highway. The moment felt surreal. Instead of panicking, my practiced faith in God's enveloping presence took over. I breathed in the Spirit and reminded myself that my God is before me and behind me and has placed His hand upon me. I asked for the details. She was safe. The other driver was safe. Her car was totaled. I felt the strong hand of my Protector rest upon me, and I realized that He would always be there. For me and for those I love. For all of us, if we allow Him to pour His presence into our lives.

Faith Step

Regular scripture memorization is a lifeline. Choose a verse that has spoken to you powerfully in the past and commit to imprint it on your soul. Print it out from your computer or write it out by hand. Make several copies and put them in places that you regularly return to throughout the day—the console of your car, your bathroom mirror, the fridge. Invite a family member or friend to join you in this practice. Every time you see the verse, reread it aloud. Then practice saying it to yourself without looking. Soon it will be yours. I guarantee it will be a treasure that will present itself at a time of need.

I Am Chosen and I Belong

LANA WYNN SCROGGINS

But now, this is what the LORD says—he who created you, Jacob, he who formed you, Israel: "Do not fear, for I have redeemed you; I have summoned you by name; you are mine."

—Isaiah 43:1, NIV

I still remember the day our parents told us we were adopted. My brother and I were sitting in the living room, surrounded by the warmth of the late afternoon sun, unaware that everything was about to change.

Mom's voice was soft, but her words hit hard. "We want to share something important with you," she began, looking at each of us with eyes full of love. My heart started racing before the words even left her mouth. "You were adopted."

I didn't know what to feel. Part of me had always known something was different, but hearing it out loud made the room shift around me. It was as if I'd been standing on solid ground one moment, and the next, it crumbled beneath my feet. I stared at the carpet, my mind swirling.

"Does that mean we're not really part of the family?" I asked quietly, my voice barely above a whisper.

Mom quickly took my hand, her grip gentle yet firm. "No, sweetie. It means we chose you. We love you, and you are just as much a part of this family as anyone else." Dad nodded beside her, adding, "We couldn't imagine our lives without you."

They tried to reassure us, but something inside me had shifted. I glanced at my brother, wondering if he felt it too. We were told we belonged, but the doubt had already begun to take root. I couldn't shake the feeling that I was a puzzle piece that didn't quite fit.

In the days that followed, those feelings only grew. The cousins were the first to find out. At my grandparents' house, we were all running around the backyard, laughing and playing as usual—until the word *adopted* slipped out. From that moment, everything changed.

The whispers started. I caught them exchanging glances, as if seeing me for the first time in a new light. One of my cousins said, "So, you're not really part of the family, huh?" The smirk stung more than I wanted to admit. I shrugged it off, but the words echoed in my mind.

After that, every comment—whether intentional or not—hit like a punch. "You don't look like the rest of us," someone said. "I guess you're not really related," another cousin joked. The more they said, the more I started to believe it. Maybe they were right. Maybe I didn't belong.

At home, I tried to hide how I felt. I didn't want to worry my parents. But one evening after dinner, my mom sat next to me on the couch, her hand resting on my shoulder. "You've been quiet lately," she said softly. "What's on your mind?"

I hesitated, then blurted out, "The cousins—they keep saying we're not really part of the family." I looked down, my voice trembling. "Maybe they're right."

Mom sighed deeply, pulling me into a hug. "Oh honey, they're not right. Not even close. Family isn't about blood; it's about love. Your dad and I chose you because we wanted you. You belong here."

Dad chimed in from the kitchen, his voice full of warmth. "We prayed for you, waited for you, and the moment we found you, we knew you were meant to be ours. That's what matters."

Their words soothed me for a while, but deep down, the doubt still lingered.

Things got harder at school. Making friends had always been a struggle, but now it felt as though there was a barrier between me and everyone else. I watched kids laughing in the hallways, sitting together at lunch, and I couldn't help but wonder if they saw me the way my cousins did.

I worked up the courage one day to sit with Debbie and her friends. She was outgoing and seemed like the kind of person everyone liked. I slid into the seat next to her, hoping to blend in. But halfway through lunch, she turned to me and said, "So, I heard you're adopted. Is that true?"

I nodded, trying to keep my face neutral. "Yeah, it's true."

"That's cool, I guess," she said with a shrug, before turning back to her conversation.

I tried to act as though it didn't matter, but all I could think about was how much I didn't fit in.

It was after one of those long, lonely days that I found myself flipping through the Bible my parents had given me. I don't know why I picked it up, but I was searching for something that would make me feel better. That's when I came across Isaiah 43:1 (NIV): "Do not fear, for I have redeemed you; I have summoned you by name; you are mine."

The words hit me like a wave. I read the verse over and over again. God has called me by name. I am His. It didn't matter if my cousins didn't accept me or if I didn't fit in at school—because I wasn't just chosen by my parents. I was chosen by God. That truth became like an anchor in the storm. Every time those doubts crept in, I repeated to myself, "I am His. I belong."

One evening, I shared the verse with my mom. "I've been thinking about what you said—that you chose me. And I've been reading this verse in Isaiah. It says that God has called me by name, that I belong to Him."

Mom smiled softly. "That's beautiful."

"It's more than beautiful," I said. "It's what I needed to hear. I don't have to be afraid anymore. I belong—not just to you and Dad but to God. And that means I'm not here by accident."

The truth of Isaiah 43:1 gave me strength I didn't know I had. But it wasn't long before that confidence was tested again.

When I decided to try out for the school tennis team, the doubts resurfaced. What if I wasn't good enough? What if I didn't fit in with the other players? While I was standing on the court for tryouts, my heart raced with fear. *You don't belong here*, the voice whispered. *You're not good enough.*

I closed my eyes and took a deep breath, remembering the words of Isaiah 43:1. "Do not fear . . . I have summoned you by name . . . you are mine." I repeated the verse in my mind, letting it wash over me. When I stepped onto the court, it wasn't just to play tennis—it was to face down the doubts that had followed me for so long.

By the end of tryouts, I made the team. And with each match I played, my confidence grew—not just in my ability but in who I was. I was chosen. I belonged. I wasn't just part of a family or a team; I was part of something much bigger. God had called me by name.

Faith Step

When you're feeling alone, scared, or unsure, remind yourself that you are chosen, loved, and you belong. God has called you by name and placed you exactly where He wants you, with the people He has chosen for you.

What Lies Ahead

CYNTHIA MENDENHALL

I focus on this one thing: Forgetting the past and looking forward to what lies ahead, I press on to reach the end of the race and receive the heavenly prize for which God, through Christ Jesus, is calling us.

—Philippians 3:13–14, NLT

Tears rolled down both cheeks as I affixed neon stickers to items once precious to me.

A judge granted me thirty days to completely vacate my home. With everything quickly packed for the ten-mile drive to my new single-again life, all those boxes, bags, and tubs now needed to be sorted. The sentimental gifts, years-old collections, and special-occasion clothes were relegated to the garage in preparation for a massive sale. There was no desire in me to see or keep the stuff of my past.

The idea of "out with the old; in with the new" proved more challenging than when I conceived the plan. A whole box of tissues perched on a table in the garage, next to a permanent marker and a roll of masking tape. The sadness overwhelmed me as I situated the relics of a thirty-year marriage and all the attached memories on display for bargain-hunting strangers to peruse and purchase.

The past is difficult to forget.

My hurt still felt fresh as I held tightly to the injustices, happy to name and blame the guilty. I plunged headfirst into victimhood and was quite content wallowing in the pain that forced this huge life change for me and my daughters. I knew I had to make a future for myself but wasn't sure how—wasn't completely sure how much I really wanted to create a new life alone.

Thankfully, God had appointed a strong mentor to walk with me through this dark and threatening journey of betrayal, rejection, and eventual divorce. Jan and I first met only four days after my world collapsed. She stayed near, checking in daily, bringing me food, and listening. She continually consoled and coached me, most often with scriptures handwritten on plain white index cards. Jan is one of those people who always operates with wisdom and discernment. Her go-to manual: the Bible. Her weapon of choice: prayer. She was tough too. She refused to allow settling in any area.

Once the morning of the advertised sale arrived, people crowded into my garage a whole hour early. Trading sentimental knickknacks and former gifts for cash brought less relief than I had hoped. I bullied myself into not crying. It was a challenge still to be friendly and kind while an emotional mess. But I knew I had to provide good customer service. Imagine if potential customers felt guilty about buying the things I no longer wanted?

As the early morning crowd subsided, Jan walked up the driveway. She brought a much-needed coffee, hot and black, just like I prefer it. She also handed me a gift bag adorned with a sunflower, overflowing with golden tissue paper.

The first item I pulled from the tissue was a notebook-sized composition book. Jan had printed a label and attached it to the front cover. I rubbed my index finger over the dark, bold letters: FUTURE.

The second part of her gift was much smaller and had slid to the bottom of the bag. It was a miniature composition notebook, identical to the large one, except it fit into the palm of my hand. Its tiny label read: PAST.

What a concrete example of perspective Jan gifted me that day!

She knew I could not live in my past and overcome it. Many of us try to do that. We cannot forget the hurt others have caused us, and we tend to hold tightly to the mistakes and messes we have made along the way as well. We keep our past close, sometimes daily clasping and polishing it, never allowing it to lose its power over us. So many people get stuck in their ideal scenarios of how life should have or could have been different. Way too often, we focus so much on the past that we do not have the energy or focus to give a thought toward plotting and planning a fascinating future.

The biblical reminder to do just that—to focus on the future and to continue running the race of my life like I planned to win it—was found inside each notebook. Jan had written out the verse in her signature cursive, adding a few key underlines: "I focus on this one thing: forgetting the past and looking forward to what lies ahead, I press on to reach the end of the race and receive the heavenly prize for which God, through Christ Jesus, is calling us" (Philippians 3:13–14, NLT).

The two notebooks presented me with a choice and a sense of urgency. A decision was needed, and this was the perfect time to make it. For the rest of my life, I could focus every day on reliving the hurts of my past. Or I could embrace the idea that God had planned a way bigger, more promising, and a whole lot more adventurous future for me.

As the sale continued, I watched as special outfits were whisked away from my wardrobe, and I wrapped valuable collectibles in newspaper and recycled grocery bags. Jan's simple gift of perspective changed everything in me that day. My internal shift was immediate and necessary. Once that switch had flipped, the memories attached to all these items no longer held the sting they had earlier.

My mind was now free to consider how fun and full my future would look. And I asked God to make it just that. It was as if I finally placed my hand in His, surrendered my fears and hurts, and whispered to Him: "Let's go!"

Jan's gift nudged me to start dreaming about that fun and full future and how I could press on in the race God has planned for me. Those verses have guided my life for almost twenty years now. And those two notebooks sit in my office as a continual reminder to keep pressing forward.

Faith Step

If you struggle with letting go of your past, create your own FUTURE and PAST notebooks. Only in coming to terms with your past will you be able to design and embrace the free, fun, and fascinating future God has planned for you.

Keep Your Eyes on God

CECIL TAYLOR

"Our God, will you not judge them? For we have no power to face this vast army that is attacking us. We do not know what to do, but our eyes are on you."

—2 Chronicles 20:12, NIV

My Haitian missionary friend was wrapping up our Zoom call. Her final statement was, "My husband and I are living on 2 Chronicles 20:12."

I smiled and nodded as if I knew the verse, but I didn't. I immediately opened my Bible, and soon afterward, I was placing the verse on a sticky note above my computer so I could always keep it at the forefront of my thinking.

Second Chronicles 20 tells of a desperate time in the history of Judah. King Jehoshaphat learns that armies from Moab, Ammon, and Mount Seir have combined to attack Judah. Realizing his nation is greatly outnumbered, Jehoshaphat wisely inquires of the Lord and proclaims a fast across the land. The people of Judah gather in Jerusalem to seek help from the Lord, and Jehoshaphat leads them in a prayer for deliverance.

Jehoshaphat concludes his prayer with these words: "We do not know what to do, but our eyes are on you."

The answer comes quickly. As everyone silently waits, the Spirit of the Lord enters a Levite, Jahaziel, who proclaims that the people of Judah only need to take positions against the invaders but will not have to fight, as the Lord will be with them.

Indeed, the next day, the army of Judah finds that the three warring nations have turned on one another, and every last opponent has been destroyed in the conflict.

Since I learned of this verse, it has become central to my spiritual life and to my teaching ministry. I have prayed many times, "I do not know what to do, but my eyes are on you." I have prayed it to start my day, whispered it in the middle of the night when stressed, and said it aloud as I considered a decision. As I await an answer, just like the people of Judah, I have confidence that God is already addressing my request.

Sometimes the answer has come as encouragement. More times than I would like to admit, I wonder if I'm doing the right thing in ministry. I become impatient and want to see progress in attracting people to read my blog or purchase my books. I tell the Lord, "I do not know what to do, but my eyes are on you."

One time I recited the phrase as I prayed for encouragement that I was following the right path. The next sales report on one of my older books surprised me. In one week, customers had purchased as many copies as in the lifespan of the book. I had no idea why this would be. There was no recent marketing effort that would have spurred such an increase. I can only attribute it to God's hand moving to encourage me.

Sometimes the phrase has changed my heart and reset my mind. On an occasion when I fretted over the financial state of my ministry, I prayed the verse. Soon, an inspiration occurred. I had been thinking about the number of customers. I felt the Spirit tugging me in another direction to think primarily about individuals rather than numbers, considering the needs of each person who would be reading and viewing my material. Realizing the impact I could bring to individual lives, I determined my daily focus should be on the one wandering sheep who needed what I had to say. That inspiration changed the way I approach my writing, blogging, and video creation.

Often the verse assists my discernment on key decisions. One of the major choices I've had to make involved switching to a new publisher. I gained the opportunity through what I can only describe as a "God appointment," sitting next to a publisher's representative on a plane. He encouraged me to submit a book proposal.

But I waffled. I wasn't sure it was the right thing. Perhaps his editorial board wouldn't accept my book idea. I was busy, so I figured a proposal would be a waste of precious time.

Through praying "I do not know what to do, but my eyes are on you," I discerned that I should go forward with the proposal.

Still, I continued to balk. The publishing board accepted the proposal, but I didn't accept the offer right away. Certain financial conditions of their contract seemed too risky to me. A mathematical sort, I created a spreadsheet of formulas and concluded that it wasn't a good deal, and I should say no.

A day before a meeting at which I intended to reject the publisher, I felt it was time for another round of "my eyes are on you." I discerned this message in return: "Go back and look at the calculations again." When I did, I realized I had made some wrong assumptions. I decided that if the publisher would commit to selling a certain quantity of books in the first two years, I would agree to the contract.

I didn't tell the publisher my secret number. When I asked the question about sales forecasts, the answer returned as the target number plus 25 percent. I was glad the Lord inspired me to check my spreadsheet again, and I accepted the deal.

You would think that I would have learned of God's overall will for me to go along with this publisher, but there have been subsequent decisions such as marketing opportunities in working with this publisher. In each case, I thought, no. But when I inquired with my eyes focused on the Lord, I've again been led to go forward with every opportunity. Instead of leaning on my own wisdom, I have kept my eyes on God when I didn't know what to do.

It is definitely not the case that the verse is a set of magic words that always draws an immediate answer. Instead, praying this verse moves my focus from earthly calculations to God's will. I'm able to better discern God's will yet am also more patient in the many times when an answer doesn't quickly appear. I have learned to trust that God is working and that I need to go forward until I catch up to what the Lord is doing.

In my personal life, this verse has been extremely useful. My wife and I pray each morning, and it's not unusual to say, "We do not know what to do, but our eyes are on you." When contemplating health concerns, wise money management, difficult personal interactions with others, or even the argument we had the night before, praying this verse brings us calm and clarity.

Looking back, I realize how often I have pursued certainty and comfort in earthly ways. God doesn't promise that kind of comfort but rather the comfort and security that you feel when God's arms are wrapped around you.

I've shared this passage with both my audience and with individuals struggling for discernment, clarity, and comfort. The looks on their faces remind me of my own reaction when hearing the phrase for the first time. Those faces reveal a mix of newfound understanding and a realization that they need to locate that verse in the Bible and read it for themselves.

Living this verse has increased my faith—not only because of the times when my questions were answered but also because

I have learned to trust that God is moving, even when I can't perceive it. I only need to keep my eyes fixed upon the Lord.

Faith Step

When uncertain, distressed, or confused, do not lean on your own wisdom or emotions. Instead, seek the Lord and say, "I do not know what to do, but my eyes are on you." Then wait expectantly in faith for guidance and peace.

I Will Not Leave You Desolate

PEGGY EASTMAN

"I will not leave you desolate; I will come to you. Yet a little while, and the world will see me no more, but you will see me; because I live, you will live also."

—John 14:18–19, RSV

When my husband, Jim, was killed in a plane crash in a wooded area of Maine, part of me wished that I had been sitting next to him. We could have wrapped our arms around each other and died together.

Two detectives came to my front door to tell me my husband was dead. Their words felt like a physical slap. I knew I could not be comforted; I felt like an emotional amputee. What did I have to live for now? Suddenly, I was a childless widow at the age of forty-three; I wanted to curl into myself and pull away from everything and everyone. An invisible shroudlike cloud descended on me.

My Aunt Ann, a Navy wife, gently pressed a little green leatherbound New Testament into my hands and told me to read John 14:18–19 (which she had underlined in pencil) over and over. I did. The little book naturally opened at this chapter, as if my aunt had read it many times. But how would Jesus come to comfort me, as scripture promised? How could He make me feel less desolate?

When my church started a bereavement support group, I wasn't sure I wanted to go. The one person in my life I counted most precious had been suddenly wrenched away from me.

How could this group help me? What did they know of my pain? I could hardly pull myself together to drive to the church, but I felt drawn to go, as if someone were softly nudging me. With hesitation, I walked into the first meeting. I could barely say my name and what had happened to me when introductions were being made because I was afraid I might cry.

But as I listened to those who had come to this group, I realized that I was not alone in my profound grief. Harry and Rudy had lost their wives. Carole had lost her brother. Helen and Tom had lost their infant son, their first child. Jan had lost her fiancé in a freak boating accident. These were my fellow members in Christ; they, too, had been devastated by loss. Others had suffered different personal losses. Just hearing their stories seemed to lighten that load of grief on my shoulders. As I listened to them talk softly about their losses, I realized over and over that I was not alone. I had not been purposely singled out for loss and grief. Jesus was keeping His word in the promise of this scripture passage: He had guided and led me to the right place. He knew I needed this group and was comforting me through others.

As I went to our weekly bereavement support meetings, we became a kind of family. We had been strangers at the beginning for the most part, but we came to share our feelings more and more freely: the pain of seeing a beloved spouse's empty chair every evening; the sorrow at having to put away the tiny blue sweater, hat, and booties for an infant son who died; the fear of being left bereft in life without parents or one's only brother; the profound pain of losing a life partner before even taking wedding vows and exchanging rings. Here tears flowed freely, and it was OK to cry. We became friends who shared a special bond. There was a box of tissues on the coffee table.

I now understood that Jesus really does keep His promises. He was not leaving me desolate; He was coming to comfort me through the sharing and care of others. As I read and reread John 14:18–19 in the little green New Testament, I became more and more convinced of how firmly we need to trust that Jesus always keeps His promises. And I came to understand that we can trust Him because of His deep, abiding love for us.

After a while, our pastor came to one of our bereavement support group meetings and asked us to write a Christian booklet on coping with grief to comfort other grievers. It seemed like an overwhelming task at first, but then I realized that I could turn my own mourning into helping others. I could become part of God's plan to comfort all His grieving children and leave none desolate. So could the other members of our group. I had a purpose larger than myself. God did not mean for me to die in the plane crash that killed my husband.

So we began. I took notes, and the other members did too. We discussed the topics we wanted to write about: feeling solitary after a devastating loss; the phases of grief and the long healing process; taking charge of our own grief; how friends could help mourners; bereavement and the Christian life. Writing this booklet by committee became a lifeline for us. Everyone contributed. I was chosen to do the final editing. Was this, too, part of the scripture passage in the book of John? Was this task part of Jesus's promise not to leave me desolate and without purpose?

As we worked on our bereavement booklet, our friendships deepened. I felt less and less alone. I looked forward every week to our meeting. We had started going sometimes to a casual nearby restaurant for hamburgers, and I looked forward to those gatherings too. There we talked about little things having nothing to do with grief: pets, work issues, house repairs, TV shows, the weather. We smiled, we laughed—and I discovered that I really could still laugh. Was this, too, part of Jesus's plan not to leave me desolate, as the scripture passage promised? To give me a social life again with friends? My husband was dead, and we would never do together what we had loved: skiing, hiking, going to concerts, grabbing a quick dinner at a café after work. But God had filled my life with new friends.

Our church published the first run of our booklet. When we held our newly published bereavement booklet in our hands, we were awed. It was as if God had used each one of us and channeled Himself through us in a special way to create this final printed product. We had all approved the title: *For They Shall Be Comforted: A Guide for Those Who Mourn a Loved One's Death and for Friends Who Want to Help*. The introduction to our booklet talked about how we had come together:

> We came not because of professional qualifications or educational backgrounds or life goals. We came because each of us had suffered from the death of someone very dear. We came, some of us, with hesitation and with a gnawing fear that it would be too painful to share our grief with others. We were afraid that, in talking about our feelings, we would only sharpen the hurt we felt. What we found instead was caring and support beyond our hopes. We found acceptance, kindness, and companionship. What we found, in short, was a new family.

Our church contracted with a religious publisher for the second run of our bereavement booklet. I bought a large quantity of them, and for years I gave this booklet for free to all those I knew who had lost a loved one. I am convinced that God had a purpose for me after my husband's death, even though I could not see it myself. I am convinced that He used this group of caring friends to persuade me that He would not leave me desolate but would bring me comfort in abundance and give me a new purpose and joy in helping to carry out His work on earth.

I also believe strongly that God has a purpose for each one of us, even though we may not know it ourselves. Life is hard, and it is full of struggles. But God will never leave any one of us desolate; He will come to each of us when we are in deep sorrow in His own way. Because Jesus lives, we will live also and have life abundantly. He always keeps His promises.

Faith Step

God is close to the brokenhearted and works through others to comfort us. When you feel sorrow, you may be tempted to withdraw, keep your pain to yourself, and suffer alone. But reaching out to others—family, friends, coworkers, and fellow Christians—allows God to provide His loving care through those who care for you.

Digging Wells of Blessings

SANDI CRUMPTON HERRON

What joy for those whose strength comes from the LORD, who have set their minds on a pilgrimage to Jerusalem. When they walk through the Valley of Weeping, it will become a place of refreshing springs. The autumn rains will clothe it with blessings.

—Psalm 84:5–6, NLT

I shoved my books, notepad, pens, and phone into my pink tote bag and waved goodbye to the nurses and technicians as I made my way down the hall.

As I approached the door leading to the parking lot, the bright red letters of the sign caught my attention. EXIT. I paused and breathed a sigh of relief. I finished my last chemo treatment today, closing this chapter of my battle against cancer. When the radiation treatments are complete, it will mark the end of this journey, and I will make my final exit.

Before the door closed, I glanced back at fellow patients, who, like me, had been unprepared for a cancer diagnosis. I began traveling this unfamiliar terrain when I discovered a lump in my breast, which doctors later confirmed as cancer.

I refer to this cancer journey as my "Valley of Baca." I would not have chosen it, but I would not change it.

Baca means "balsam" but is also the Hebrew word meaning "to weep." The Valley of Baca is often referred to as "the Valley of Weeping."

When the unexpected happens in our lives, we can find ourselves in a valley of weeping. Not only cancer but also other challenges—financial difficulties, relationship problems—can cause a shift in our lives and bring pain and heartache. Defeat, failure in business, a shattered marriage, or the death of a loved one sends us into what appears to be a never-ending spiral of grief. Often, these things come into our lives like a dust storm that blocks the sun, leaving us gasping for air and frantically searching for cover.

Psalm 84, written by David as a song of worship, describes pilgrims who passed through a dry and parched valley, determined to reach Mount Zion in Jerusalem, their place of worship. The travelers dug wells along the way, and when the autumn rains came, the wells filled with fresh water, serving as nourishing pools for others who came later.

The Hebrew word for *pool* means "blessing." The wells we dig when we are in a place of pain and suffering become wells of blessings for others.

When my journey began, fear, anxiety, and loneliness consumed me, but I soon found hope, strength, and nourishment from the wells of experience that were dug by those who had gone before me.

Often, the things we do for others will impact us in ways we never expect. My valley of weeping became a place of joy as I dug wells to encourage and nourish others.

While taking my first chemo treatment, I made eye contact with a lady sitting across from me. We smiled at each other, and, before leaving, I introduced myself.

During my next visit, we sat across from each other again. I rolled my IV pump with me and walked over to where she sat. Up close, I could see the sorrow in her eyes. We talked, and when I shared a humorous story with her, we found ourselves in deep laughter. Before leaving, she stopped, gently squeezed my arm, and whispered, "Thank you for making me laugh. I have not laughed in months. You made me feel that there is hope."

My new friend did not realize it, but she gave me hope that day as well. As I left the cancer center, I thanked God for placing me right where He wanted me at that time of my life—fighting cancer and digging wells. Sharing hope.

From that day forward, digging wells in my Valley of Baca became my purpose.

At times, I could not see the path ahead, but I knew God always kept His promises. When my "normal" life became unrecognizable, placing my faith and trust in God changed how I responded to my circumstances. Remembering what He had done in the past gave me hope for the future. With determination, I dug wells of faith and filled them with the promises of God's Word.

The day my hair came out, my husband dug a well and filled it with the blessing of tears when he wrapped his arms around me and let me cry. He didn't say, "It's only hair," because he understood what it symbolized, and the hurt was deep. He held me tight, and it was as if God was wrapping me in a warm blanket, telling me He understood my tears.

On a chilly November morning, when a young girl in a drive-through window mistook the wig in my lap for a puppy, an ordinary wig got a new name: Fido. If the young girl faces a time when a wig is part of her life story, perhaps she will remember that laughter is medicine for wounded hearts. In a drive-through window, we dug a well and filled it with the blessings of laughter.

Many people dug wells and filled them with the blessings of friendship when they sent cards, brought food, and stopped for visits. Their actions let me know I was not alone. In turn, I dug a well of praise and filled it with prayers for those encouraging me.

When I allowed my young granddaughters to draw on my bald head, I took away their fears as we dug a well and filled it with the blessing of joy. Someday, when they face hard times, they will recall how their grandmother faced a frightening time of life but showed them how to live and find joy right where they are. I showed them that God doesn't wait for us to come to the top of the mountain; He meets us in our valley.

While on vacation in Arizona, my family and I climbed to the top of one of the highest mountain peaks. Because of my rush to get to the top, I suddenly became lightheaded and could not focus. Those around me were enjoying the view, but I was struggling to breathe. When my son recognized I had altitude sickness, he instructed me to breathe slowly and deeply. Once we descended the mountain and reached the valley below, I could easily breathe again.

On the mountaintop, while enjoying the view, it's easy to miss the struggles of those around us. But, in the valley, we are aware of the needs of others and dig wells to make a difference.

Like the pilgrims in the Valley of Baca, traveling to a place of worship, our valley takes us into the presence of God, where He showers us with grace and gives us strength to fulfill our purpose. When I dug wells for others, my valley became a place of refreshing and my pain was clothed with blessings.

Today, I am still digging wells and living a life cancer-free.

Faith Step

Are you facing a challenging time in your life? Find people who are also struggling and discover ways you can make a difference. When you focus on helping others—digging wells of blessings—your journey becomes a place of joy.

Living in Light of Eternity

LAURA BAILEY

He has made everything beautiful in its time. He has also set eternity in the human heart; yet no one can fathom what God has done from beginning to end.

—Ecclesiastes 3:11, NIV

As I stared in the mirror, mindlessly applying makeup, masking fine lines, covering up blemishes, and brightening my features, I couldn't help but wish I could do the same for my life. On the outside, my life checked all the right boxes. I should have felt joy and delight, yet I was miserable.

Just as I believed that a daily drop of "magic" face cream would radically erase wrinkles on my face, I fell for the same lie in my life. Climbing the corporate ladder, purchasing the big house, marrying the dream guy, hitting the magic number on the scale—I wholeheartedly believed that if I did all these things, I would find lasting contentment. But I didn't.

Until one day when God used a friend to speak to my heart and make me realize that although as a young child, I accepted God as Savior, I hadn't fully surrendered to Him as Sovereign over my life. I wanted all the benefits of a relationship with Jesus but still to live life for myself, to follow my own rules and to have one foot in the world. Graciously, the Holy Spirit exposed my divided heart as the source of the tension I'd been experiencing the last few years. The life I worked tirelessly to orchestrate wasn't what God planned for me. Unable to dismiss God's call on my life, I prayed, "I am tired of doing things my way. I submit to You and Your plan."

I knew there were quite a few things I needed to change in my life, but one of the areas the Lord was calling me to consider was my time spent in the Word. I'd read the Bible off and on over the years but never consistently. However, I knew it would take a daily renewal of mind through a consistent study of the Scriptures to submit and surrender to the Lord's will.

I've always been drawn to the book of Ecclesiastes. Perhaps it's my realistic approach to life; my glasses are far from rose-colored, and sugarcoating hard truths has never been my style. I appreciate Solomon's unapologetic observations of life in a fallen world, and I even find a bit of satisfaction in how Solomon tells it like it is. Solomon not only sees the difficulty humanity faces but also draws attention to it. However, I will concede that on the surface, especially if only sections of Ecclesiastes are read, the book has a doom-and-gloom vibe.

If Ecclesiastes's verses were cherry-picked—or perhaps if someone only read certain sections—then they could feel like a rant of a regretful, depressed man. However, the more I learned about Solomon's story, observations, warnings, and general life advice, the more I related to Solomon and his quest for lasting joy. And like Solomon, I spent years investing in the temporary over the eternal, distracted by the world's definition of success. But no matter what I did, I couldn't hold on to the peace I so desperately craved. The problem was that I was trying to get permanent peace from temporary things.

The first part of Ecclesiastes chapter 3 is one of the most quoted passages in both secular and sacred circles. I can easily relate to the different seasons of our lives that change on a whim, with or without our permission. While these verses are profound on their own, the verses that follow have guided me to understand better why I experienced tension in my faith. We live in a "now and not yet" reality.

As I read Ecclesiastes 3:11, I recognize the truth—I feel as if something is missing in my life because it is! Though I have been made new in Christ, I am not wholly restored until I go to be with my Lord and Savior in eternity. It explains why I am never satisfied when trying to find temporal contentment. My appetite is somewhat satiated, but my desires are never truly quenched. So I find myself jumping back into the rat race, searching for the next big thing I hope will finally grant me lasting fulfillment. Like Solomon, I deny myself nothing, but am I any better off at the end of the day? The answer is a resounding no.

When I started living in light of eternity, always remembering that I am simply a sojourner passing through on the way to my eternal home, I began to let go of things that have no lasting significance and cling to what truly matters. I began doing the hard work of examining my heart's motivation for my actions. Was I saying yes to "good things" in my life that came at a cost to my spiritual, emotional, and physical well-being? Was I pursuing temporary ease or comfort instead of a deeper relationship with God? I stopped trying to hustle, claw, and secure my purpose, worth, identity, and meaning. Instead, I find peace in surrendering control over my life; my life is meant to point others to Christ.

Living in light of eternity isn't always easy. But with the proper perspective, I learn to live well, fulfill my purpose to know God and make Him known, and look forward to the day I will be in His presence for all eternity.

Faith Step

For many, we've become good at practicing a "checklist Christianity." We say and do all the "right" things, yet our hearts are divided. Take time today to look at where you spend your time and resources. Are you investing in the temporary or the eternal?

To Whom Shall We Go?

ALICE J. WISLER

From this time many of his disciples turned back and no longer followed him. "You do not want to leave too, do you?" Jesus asked the Twelve. Simon Peter answered him, "Lord, to whom shall we go? You have the words of eternal life. We have come to believe and to know that you are the Holy One of God."

—John 6:66–69, NIV

Where am I? The roads all looked the same. I made a right turn and another. At a stop sign, I waited too long; the driver behind me honked. My knee-jerk reaction swung the minivan to a sharp left. The minutes ticked by on the dashboard clock. I was not only lost but also late.

Since high school, I'd prided myself on punctuality, but that day I was twenty-seven minutes late and counting. The directions I'd been given over the phone were useless after I'd made multiple wrong turns. I had no way to call; it was long before cell phones. Anxiety consumed me, but at least I knew one thing for sure: I would not ask Jesus for guidance. When darkness settled, I might still be searching for my friend's house, but I would not surrender and seek wisdom.

Before February 2, 1997, I would have pulled over to the side of one of the unfamiliar roads and asked Jesus to help me navigate to my destination. I used to talk to Jesus often, praying for friends and family, laying out my petitions before Him, and thanking Him for His presence in my life. But things had changed. As I drove through the streets, looking for an avenue or lane on my handwritten directions, all I could hear was a little bald boy asking Jesus to heal his boo-boo.

A year earlier, our three-year-old son, Daniel, was diagnosed with a malignant tumor, turning our world upside down. During a hospital stay, Daniel had wanted me to take him to the chapel. Once there, he'd lowered himself to his knees and prayed aloud for Jesus to make him well and for his hair to grow back. It was a tender moment, and I was certain Jesus heard this little boy in yellow Looney Tunes pajamas and would use the chemo and surgeries to remove the cancer cells from his body.

Instead of health, our precious child died—not from cancer but from a staph infection. My husband, daughter, son, and I were devastated. After each day of tending to the needs of my children (I was also six months pregnant), I crawled into bed, exhausted and tearful. In my journal, I poured out my grief. *Why Lord? How come? Why wasn't there a plan for Daniel to have a future on Earth? What happened to all those prayers we prayed? Why pray at all? How can I ever trust You again?*

Our church didn't know how to handle our sorrow. Many congregants wondered why I wasn't my happy self. Some wanted me to put on a smile and just be glad Daniel was in heaven with Jesus.

My husband's coworker gave us a book filled with accounts written by bereaved Christian parents. One testimony was from Caralie, a mother who had lost her three-year-old son forty years before to the same cancer Daniel had—neuroblastoma. Reading her bio, I saw she lived in the next town, so I got her number from the phone book and called her. When Caralie answered, I briefly told her my story, and she invited me for lunch the next week. Eager to talk with another mother who had been through agony, I arranged childcare for my toddler. My eldest would be in her first-grade class at school.

I had not expected to get lost on the way to Caralie's house. But when I finally got to her front door, the elderly woman hugged me and didn't seem to mind that I was an hour tardy.

Sitting down to a tuna casserole she had kept warm in the oven, we shared about our boys. When she cried, I knew that even after forty years—should I live so long—I would still mourn the hole in my heart caused by the absence of my son.

Caralie did not scold me for my doubts. She let me ask the tough questions, similar to the ones I posed in my journal. She told me God can handle our frustration and confusion. Countless psalms are filled with laments to God.

Shortly after our baby was born, our family found another church to attend. There, we met families who had also buried children, and they embraced our vulnerability and invited us into their homes. Feeling acknowledged and accepted were blessings.

At a Bible study, we read the passage where Jesus asked his disciples if they wanted to leave Him. Other followers of His weren't able to handle some of His more challenging teachings and turned away. "You do not want to leave too, do you?" Jesus questioned the Twelve.

Oh, yes! I thought. You know I have wanted to leave. I wanted a Savior who would have allowed my son to live. I wanted my ways, my blueprints. I'd expected Jesus to spare me from suffering. In the passage, Peter replied to Jesus, "To whom shall we go?" The question leaped from the page into my soul. *Where would I go? Who else is there?*

I'd been a believer since I was sixteen when I experienced a peace that passes all understanding and begged for the presence of Jesus to stay with me forever. Jesus had been with me when I was in college ten thousand miles away from my missionary parents; when, as a young adult, I taught refugees at a rustic camp in the Philippines; when I prayed for a husband and got married; when my children were born; and when Daniel was diagnosed. Throughout the years, I knew I belonged to the One who gave His life for me.

Losing my child pulled me away from trusting Jesus. But not for long. I invited the Lord to walk with me again. Eventually, my doubts and questions subsided as my love for Him expanded. I accepted God as not only a God of mystery but also a God who increases our faith so that we trust Him even during times of uncertainty and grief. Who else had the words of hope, mercy, forgiveness, and grace I needed to hear? Who else accepted me in my frailty and sin? Who else filled the deep crevices of my heart? Who else knew me through and through and still loved me?

Yes, Holy One of God, it's only You! Thank You for the endless life I have with You.

Faith Step

When you're going through a difficult season and find yourself doubting Jesus, consider Simon Peter's words in John 6. Remind yourself of Jesus's everlasting love for you.

The Greatest of These

HEATHER JEPSEN

Now these three remain: faith, hope and love. But the greatest of these is love.

—1 Corinthians 13:13, NIV

Many people are familiar with this passage of scripture. We often read it at weddings assuming that the Apostle Paul was writing about the love between couples and families. But the true historical nature of this text is that Paul was writing it to a church in conflict. This is about how people who are not family find a way to get along and be the church together. And that way is love.

I have been in ministry for twenty years, and I have never known a church that did not have conflict of some sort. It is just a natural part of getting together a group of people with varying backgrounds and interests. I always teach that even though we feel as if we choose a specific church to attend, the reality is that God brings us together. God chooses our church for us, and God has a plan for this specific group of people, even when we can't always tell what that plan is.

One of the most difficult conflicts I have experienced in a congregation was when I had my first child. I was serving as a solo pastor in a small town with a small church. About forty people attended worship every week, and I was the only paid person on staff. Everyone else, from song leader to janitor, was a volunteer. We had developed a good balance of working together, but everything would change when my baby was born.

I'm not sure what set things off, but when I returned from my maternity leave (of only four weeks), I endured one of the roughest patches of my entire ministry career. Suddenly, it seemed as though everyone was mad at me, and nothing I was doing was good enough. Plus, personally I was struggling at home. Those who have had children know that those first few months with a new baby can be really hard. It is a steep learning curve, and there is not much opportunity for rest and sleep, so admittedly I was not at 100 percent either.

My first sign something was amiss was when I neglected to go to an extra evening event. The church was hosting a touring bicycle group with a barbecue dinner, and I decided to skip the event and stay home. I figured they didn't really need to have the pastor there, and I had a newborn. Well, I figured wrong.

The next morning, several members were in my office. "Where were you last night? Why weren't you at the event?" I replied that I thought they could do it without me and that my baby needed me at home. "You are using that baby as an excuse not to work," one woman spat back. I was stunned. What does that even mean? And how could a little church lady be so cruel to a new mother?

I apologized, promised to do better, and escorted the women out of the office. Alone again, I prayed. *Lord, what am I doing wrong? How am I supposed to balance all these things?*

The anger continued in the congregation with snide side comments and hostile glares. Technically, I was doing all that was required of me, everything in my job description. But naturally, I couldn't go above and beyond as I had before; I had a baby girl at home now. My workload just had to look different.

The worst day was when I got a sitter and drove with a church friend to a larger church meeting an hour away. We had enjoyed a lovely day together with worship, business, and lunch. On the way back to our small town, suddenly the woman I thought was my friend started to let loose.

"You know, you should quit this job. It's time for you to leave. Everyone is upset since you had the baby. We actually paid for you to have that baby anyway." I was dumbstruck. I just nodded and tried to keep driving without crying.

"Thanks for letting me know," I replied as my heart broke. I thought this person was my friend. I just couldn't understand where all the anger was coming from.

When I got back home, I grabbed my baby girl and cuddled her close. I had missed her while I was gone. And I couldn't believe that such an innocent little baby could cause such conflict in my church. Weren't churches supposed to be about love, kindness, and grace?

As I hugged my baby, reflecting on love, the words of 1 Corinthians 13:4 (NIV) came to me: "Love is patient, love is kind. It does not envy, it does not boast, it is not proud." Even though my heart was breaking, even though my feelings were hurt, still I could be patient with this church, couldn't I? I still had room to be kind.

I thought and prayed and read my Bible. I began to realize that congregations with female pastors sometimes develop a mother/child relationship. My congregants were acting like they were my children. And I imagined they were worried that I wouldn't love them anymore now that I had a real child of my own. This church, because it was small, had had many pastors who only stayed for one or two years. I think they were worried that I would leave them, and they wanted to push me away first. *Well*, I thought to myself, *that's not how love works.*

I weathered the storm. I stayed, I let all the hurtful words go, and I modeled servant leadership as best I could by forgiving them. *They don't really mean it*, I told myself. *They are just afraid.*

Conflict will always be part of life in the church. And when we are in the middle of it, in the deep depths of hurtful words and misunderstanding, love is what gets us through. Love can look like acts of service, putting others before ourselves and offering forgiveness so the community can remain intact. Love is what helps us move forward when faith is in doubt and hope seems far away.

The Apostle Paul was right when he wrote this famous letter to his church in conflict. We need faith and we need hope, but it is love that will get us through. It is love that we need to be the people of God. And that's why the greatest of these is love.

Faith Step

What act of love might God be calling you to today? Is there someone you need to forgive? A hurt you need to let go of? A place in your community where you can smooth conflict? How can you act in the love of God this day?

Earnestly Seeking God

CAROLINE S. COOPER

O God, You are my God; I shall seek You earnestly; my soul thirsts for You, my flesh yearns for You, in a dry and weary land where there is no water. Thus I have seen You in the sanctuary, to see Your power and Your glory. Because Your lovingkindness is better than life, my lips will praise You. So I will bless You as long as I live; I will lift up my hands in Your name. My soul is satisfied as with marrow and fatness, and my mouth offers praises with joyful lips. When I remember You on my bed, I meditate on You in the night watches, for You have been my help, and in the shadow of Your wings I sing for joy. My soul clings to You; Your right hand upholds me.

—Psalm 63:1–8, NASB1995

"God, I hear you."

Sobbing, I crawled out from the covers and fell to the floor. The curtains in the bedroom I shared with my husband of twenty years could not block out the afternoon sun. How long had I been lying there? A few hours? Maybe a few days? The late summer months had blurred together as I spent an increasing amount of time in my room, hiding from my family and my past.

I had left my room at times to prove I was a good mom to our four children who ranged in age from seven to fourteen. And I dared not miss attending church with my family. I even continued to teach a children's Bible study. I had to keep up appearances. No one needed to know the brokenness I experienced. No one needed to know that behind closed doors my husband felt helpless, and my kids had learned to care for themselves.

On that September day in 2002, God's still small voice broke through my tears. I had almost forgotten what it sounded like. The Spirit overwhelmed me as I bowed down and implored God to take away my deep depression and mood swings. I pleaded for Him to remove the guilt and shame I felt over my depression that threatened to destroy my marriage. He whispered, "I love you. You are not alone." For the first time in weeks, I knew what to do.

With the assistance of a therapist, I got the help I needed. And I began to turn to the psalms for comfort. I could relate to the Psalmists who cried out for help. When I read Psalm 63, I knew God had brought it to my attention to guide me through the recovery process.

O God, You are my God; I shall seek You earnestly; my soul thirsts for You, my flesh yearns for You, in a dry and weary land where there is no water (Psalm 63:1, NASB1995).

My treatment began in a ten-day outpatient program in the trauma unit of a psychiatric hospital. I shared David's sentiment of being in a desert land and looked forward to God providing life-giving water to quench my parched and hopeless soul. I learned I had post-traumatic stress disorder (PTSD) from childhood trauma and bipolar depression. God saved my life in that facility. I knew I had to seek Him with my whole being every step of the way.

Thus I have seen You in the sanctuary, to see Your power and Your glory. Because Your lovingkindness is better than life, my lips will praise You (Psalm 63:2–3, NASB1995).

Each day, I attended therapy, pored over workbooks, and practiced new skills for improving my mental health. The shame that had kept me prisoner started to dissolve, and I recalled how God had sustained me in the past. I knew God would now provide the power for me to persevere through the ups and downs of recovery. His overwhelming love surrounded me, and I began to turn my sorrow into praise.

So I will bless You as long as I live; I will lift up my hands in Your name (Psalm 63:4, NASB1995).

When the ten-day program ended, I rejoiced in the Lord for what He had taught me. I said goodbye to my fellow patients who had inspired me and encouraged me. I no longer felt alone in my challenges. Some of the women were also Christians, and we enjoyed opportunities for fellowship and prayer. But I hoped I would not share the fate of those who were regular patients in the trauma unit, sometimes being admitted multiple times in one year. I surrendered my recovery to the Lord and, like it or not, I knew I would return here if necessary.

My soul is satisfied as with marrow and fatness, and my mouth offers praises with joyful lips (Psalm 63:5, NASB1995).

After leaving the psychiatric facility, I continued in intensive therapy. I worked with a Christian therapist for a couple of years, resolving issues from my past that had been pushed far back in my memory. We used eye movement desensitization and reprocessing (EMDR), talk therapy, and prayer to help me accept my unchangeable past, resolve unhealthy coping behaviors, and learn to enjoy life. She provided affirmations for retraining my mind from negative and harmful thoughts to more positive and uplifting reflections. Each affirmation included scripture.

When my intensive treatment ended, I responded to God's nudge to share my experience with others. God stirred in my spirit to apply to seminary to prepare for ministry. When the acceptance letter came, I fell to my knees in surprise and gratitude. I had not felt worthy, but God reminded me of my worth in His eyes.

I started a mental health ministry in 2005 by turning my journals into a workbook for others who were struggling with trauma and mental illness. Shortly after, I started a mental health support group at my church and began speaking about my recovery.

I graduated from seminary in 2009 with a degree in Bible and theology after taking several classes on biblical counseling. God had faithfully brought me through treatment and blessed me richly with a full and productive life. I sang His praises in response.

When I remember You on my bed, I meditate on You in the night watches, for You have been my help, and in the shadow of Your wings I sing for joy (Psalm 63:6–7, NASB1995).

When I first read verses six and seven of Psalm 63, I immediately felt relief and a connection with the words. From childhood, I had trouble sleeping and endured strange dreams that would leave me confused and depressed. During the recovery process, I began using my time in bed to focus on God's presence, recite scripture, and listen to worship music.

A couple of years ago, in the fall of 2022, God led me to a new psychiatric nurse practitioner. She recommended a medication that would not only treat my bipolar depression but also would help me sleep. Since that time, I have slept better than any other time in my life. Now, when I'm tucked into my bed, I rest in the shadow of His wings, listening to instrumental worship music. I drift into sleep a short time after hitting the pillow. Thank You, Lord.

My soul clings to You; Your right hand upholds me (Psalm 63:8, NASB1995).

Living with a mental illness is like riding a roller coaster. Some days are great, other days not so much. Over the years I've changed medications several times. I've had depressive episodes that stretched for weeks. And, as I've grown older, I have begun experiencing more anxiety. Recovery is a lifelong journey, at least for me and most people I know who have similar stories. But I'm OK with that! My God is with me. And, I have an amazing eternal future to look forward to regardless of what happens here on this earth.

While I'm here, I will cling to the Lord. I will rely on Him to sustain and uplift me. And I will continue to serve Him in a ministry I would not have chosen for myself.

Faith Step

Even those without a clinical diagnosis may experience periods of depression and anxiety. Spending time with the Lord, knowing Him intimately, and reading His Word can provide the spiritual foundation we need when faced with heartache and trials. Despite our circumstances, we can experience joy in the Lord, comfort through the Holy Spirit, and saving grace in Christ.

Loving Your Neighbor

KENDRA ROEHL

"Teacher, which is the most important commandment in the law of Moses?" Jesus replied, "'You must love the Lord your God with all your heart, all your soul, and all your mind.' This is the first and greatest commandment. A second is equally important: 'Love your neighbor as yourself.' The entire law and all the demands of the prophets are based on these two commandments."

—Matthew 22:36–40, NLT

Do you know your literal neighbors? Do you know their names? How about any details about their lives?" our pastor asked one Sunday morning as he taught on the greatest command Jesus gave: love God and love your neighbor. I paused taking notes as I looked up, pondering his question. My husband and I first heard this idea only a few weeks earlier at a training for Christian leaders, where we were challenged to get to know and build relationships with those who lived closest to us, and this was a confirmation I felt God wanted me to hear.

I glanced at my husband, Kyle, seeing him deep in thought. "What if Jesus actually meant our literal neighbors? Not just the figurative idea of a neighbor?" our pastor asked.

I let out a sigh as conviction as his question rested on me. As we left the service, my husband squeezed my hand. We talked on the way home about all the people who lived closest to us. *Could we remember their names? What did they do for work?* If I'm honest, it was a struggle, and I only knew a couple of names, nothing more.

"Let's pray and ask God what we should do," Kyle suggested. "The Holy Spirit convicts and doesn't condemn. This isn't something we thought about before, but now that we are, let's see where God leads."

I nodded in agreement. He was right. Over the next few weeks, we began to pray and ask God for opportunities to interact with and get to know our neighbors. It started with simple "hellos" across the street when we were outside working in our yards. One night, Kyle walked over to our elderly neighbor Al's house when he sat outside to enjoy the summer evening—a habit we'd noticed, but we had never initiated a conversation with him before. He came home to tell me more details about Al—how long he'd lived in his house, what he'd done for work before retiring, and how he liked to golf.

"It was so nice. I told him we should go golfing sometime," Kyle said excitedly.

"That's great, honey," I responded.

"I've also been thinking we should host a neighborhood party," he said.

"OK," I said hesitantly.

This was one suggestion our pastor had shared as a way to get to know others. "Most people just want an invitation," he'd encouraged. I knew it was true, but being an introvert, I knew I would feel intimidated by having a yard full of people I didn't know.

"Let's ask our friends from church to assist us," Kyle said, sensing my unease. "You know they'd love to help."

"OK," I agreed. That did sound easier.

Over the next week, we picked a date and bought invitations that Kyle and our kids brought to our neighbors one evening after dinner.

"Most people were excited and said they'd love to come," he told me when they got home.

I smiled, grateful for his willingness to step out in faith with me. As the night of our neighborhood party approached, I prayed that God would use us and the time to deepen our relationships with our neighbors. I reread Matthew 22:36–40, focusing on Jesus's greatest commandment to love. And I felt peace in knowing that we were taking the steps of obedience that God was calling us to do.

The night of the party, our friends from church showed up early to set up tables and chairs, grill food, and greet neighbors as they came. Everyone brought a dish to share, and name tags made it easier to remember names. As we talked about where people lived, the makeup of their families, and what they did for work, I couldn't help but smile. I felt God's presence.

As the sun set, people became more comfortable; kids played games and ran through the yard while adults conversed in groups. It was a few hours before the first people began to gather their things to head home, thanking us for taking the initiative to host a neighborhood party, the first in our neighborhood we'd learn.

That evening opened the door to our relationship with neighbors in a whole new way. Soon, we were having dinner with our neighbors Roger and Susan, who lived across the street from us and whose adult children and grandchildren lived states away. We found they loved to play games, just as we did, and we set up regular dinners and game nights.

Jogging across the street to visit Al in the evenings also became a regular occurrence. As a widower with no children, Al built a strong relationship not just with us but also with our kids, who would often stop over to say hi or ride their bikes around his driveway while he watched from his lawn chair. Over the next few years, we held more neighborhood parties, game nights, dinners, birthday parties for our kids, and impromptu gatherings in the driveway.

We found community and friendship with those who lived closest to us. We had fun but also supported one another when hard news of a diagnosis came, family members passed away, or challenging family dynamics were shared. We were able to offer comfort and prayer because we had genuinely come to care for and love our neighbors.

Today, we no longer live in the same neighborhood, nor do many of our neighbors, but we still keep in contact. Al now lives in elderly housing; we just celebrated his ninetieth birthday with a meal from his favorite restaurant, homemade cards, and a gift with all the pictures from our times together over the years. We are so blessed to have Al not only as a neighbor or friend but also as close as a family member. He encourages and loves our kids, a bonus grandpa they are grateful to have.

When we started to initiate getting to know our neighbors, I thought we were doing it to be obedient to God's leading and to be a blessing to others. I failed to realize that I would be blessed by loving others. I would be comforted and supported. God brought us to relationships that we needed. And that is the greatest gift we've received by loving our neighbors.

Faith Step

Ask God for an opportunity to engage with one of your neighbors this week. What begins as a way to follow Jesus's command may lead to a loving and fulfilling relationship for you and your neighbor.

The A-Team

LAURA LEE LEATHERS

Now to Him who is able to do exceedingly abundantly above all that we ask or think, according to the power that works in us, to Him be glory in the church by Christ Jesus to all generations, forever and ever. Amen.

—Ephesians 3:20–21, NKJV

Today, still wanted by the government, they survive as soldiers of fortune. If you have a problem, if nobody can help, and if you can find them, maybe you can hire the A-Team.

Those were the opening words to the television program *The A-Team*, which began in January 1983 and ended in March 1987. Hannibal Smith, the fictional team leader, ensured each member implemented their part of the plan, and the A-Team always saved the day.

I had a problem—a dilemma. But I didn't need the television characters from *The A-Team* to devise a strategy of how to get the bad guys, solve the mystery, or rescue me. I needed God's A-Team, available 24/7, to answer my call and provide direction.

In March 2020, because of the pandemic, my employer sent everyone home for almost three months with pay. During that time, I was more involved in my mother's caregiving and could devote more time to writing.

When the notice came that it was time to return to work, unrest cropped into my soul. I sensed that the Lord was leading me in a different direction, to stay home. But the unknown created an anxious, fearful spirit within me.

Repeatedly, I asked myself, *Is this my desire to leave this place of employment, or is the Lord leading me in a different direction?* As I sought the Lord's path, I decided to begin a weekly practice of prayer and fasting; Wednesday became my designated day. I would read scripture, pray, and journal. I firmly believe that God always speaks through His Word and affirms His guidance through people and circumstances. From June to August, I fasted every Wednesday and considered that God was calling me to retire. But I was afraid to take such a bold step. In prayer, I often reminded the Lord that I still needed an income.

One Sunday afternoon in August, while scrolling Facebook, I noticed that an acquaintance reposted a remote job opportunity with Samaritan's Purse. I went to their website and applied for the position. Several weeks later, I received a letter from the human resources department outlining the next steps.

The Lord was opening a door. Should I wait to submit my resignation until I knew I had the job? Or simply be obedient to what He had shown me? Wanting to be obedient and trusting the Lord, I turned in my letter of resignation for October 30 before knowing I had the job. Around the middle of that month, I learned I was hired, with a start date of November 2.

Once again, in God's timing, He showed me that He could do abundantly more than I had asked. I believe that is why it is important for me to memorize, write the verses repeatedly in my journal, and share them at the end of my emails. I must remember that He is available no matter what I face.

By faith, I am learning to depend upon His power and His promises. The six words in the passage Ephesians 3:20–21 that begin with the letter *A* are powerful ones you and I can rely on. Let's briefly unpack the reason why I call them God's A-Team.

Able. God is able. There is nothing that He can't do according to His plan and will. When I study scripture and look at the times this phrase is used, I must remember that the word *impossible* is not in God's vocabulary.

For example, God provided a lamb for Abraham at the exact moment when his knife was raised. Jeremiah reminded the Israelites there was nothing too hard for God to accomplish.

Abundantly. Jesus willingly gave His life so that I might have eternal life (John 10:10), which is abundant life. He also gives me everything I need to live a life of godliness (2 Peter 1:3). To live abundantly is to live by His sustaining grace.

Above. When going through a difficult situation, I logically try to put together what it will take to solve the problem. But God takes it to a higher level. Why? Because in His Sovereignty, He knows my yesterdays, today, and tomorrows—what is best for me.

Moreover, the Bible states that everything is under His feet. My problems and situations may be above my head, but I know they are under His feet. In other words, He's got whatever I'm going through—joys and trials.

All. Perhaps this three-letter word is one of the most powerful words in scripture. It means everything; nothing is left out! Furthermore, since I am a follower of Christ, all His abundant grace is available to me. He offers sufficiency in all things (2 Corinthians 9:8).

Ask. I'm an independent person and do many things on my own. I hesitate to ask for help unless I get desperate. But that is not Jesus's instruction. He told me to ask, seek, and knock (Matthew 7:7). In the book of James, the writer tells us to ask in faith, without doubting (James 1:6). I am still working on this.

According to. The older I grow, the more I realize I have no control or authority over anything. With this word, look at the entire phrase: "according to the power that works in us." And what is that power? It is the power of the Holy Spirit. The Holy Spirit's job is to teach us the fear of the Lord and give us knowledge, wisdom, understanding, counsel, and discernment. The Holy Spirit's power equips me with the spiritual strength and courage to move faithfully into the unknown.

Why is God willing to send His A-Team to my rescue, no matter the situation? The answer is simple: to give Him glory.

The Apostle Paul's prayer tells the hearer to pray with great expectations. God is willing to send His A-Team, arriving on His timetable and according to His will. For me, in this situation, He provided a remote job, a paying staff position in my church, the ability to provide care for my aging parent, and new opportunities to write.

At the show's end, Hannibal would say, "I love it when a plan comes together!" I, too, have a catchphrase: *I love praying and seeing God's plan come together!*

Faith Step

Facing difficult life decisions and not sure where to turn? I encourage you to turn to the Lord first, delve into scripture, and pray Ephesians 3:14–21. Then wait for His timing and continue to depend upon His power and promises. God is gracious and faithful.

Cast Your Cares on Him

WENDY KLOPFENSTEIN

Cast all your anxiety on him because he cares for you.

—1 Peter 5:7, NIV

"Sis, I got it. I got the contract!" I held the phone away from my ear as she shouted with joy. She knew it was my dream to have a novel published.

My sister peppered me with questions. "What happens next? When are you going to Florida?"

"I haven't read all the information yet. I've been too excited." I couldn't keep from smiling. "Let me finish going through everything they sent, and we'll talk later."

We said our goodbyes and hung up, planning to celebrate my first publishing contract for a novel later in the week.

My eyes blurred with tears of joy as I stared back at the email.

When I'd first opened the publisher's response to my submission, I expected to see the following words: "Thank you for your submission. Better luck next time."

But that's not what it said.

And now I was reading through all the instructions about what would happen next. I'd auditioned with a publishing company to work with a well-known author, writing a story with three other authors set in the same series. My dream of having a novel published was coming true. The contracts were emailed and signed. While I was going through the process in a daze of amazement and thanksgiving, I pushed the part that terrified me to the back of my mind.

Every author in the series was required to attend a brainstorming session together for a week in Florida. I looked forward to getting to know them all as we plotted out this new series. It sounded wonderful to spend all that time with other writers by the ocean.

Everything but the part about flying there.

After a flurry of emails, the plane tickets were booked.

I stared at the information they sent me. As panic began to roll over me, I took a deep breath. Then another. Nothing squelched the rising panic inside me. It didn't help that the last time I'd flown, a tube of lip balm triggered a search of my purse that almost made me miss my flight. I dreaded the whole process of going through the airport and flying, especially alone.

"I don't know if I can do this." The words escaped me one evening as I was spending time with my sister.

"I'm sure you will be fine. It will be worth it." My sister tried her best to reassure me.

She'd even managed to borrow a carry-on suitcase for me that fit all the airline's dimension requirements—dimensions I'd studied on the airline's website as if I were studying for an exam. I didn't want to get anything wrong.

Since I hadn't flown in fifteen years, I googled everything I could think of in preparation for the flight. Unlike some people, it's not the actual flying in the plane that unnerves me. Being suspended in midair, staring out at the clouds from my window seat, never bothered me. It's all the pieces leading up to that point that fill me with hundreds of questions. Questions that read like a list of everything that could go wrong.

What if my luggage is searched? What if my luggage is lost? What if *I'm* searched? Will I make it to my gate on time? Will they bump me from my flight? What are the latest security rules? What if I come down with a debilitating migraine while in the airport? The list of questions went on and on until I'd worked myself into a frenzy.

One night, about a week before I was to fly out, I stopped scrolling the Internet, leaving behind my vast search history on planes, airports, and luggage. I put my phone down. The stillness settled around me as I began to pray.

"Lord, I know You did this. You opened the door for this opportunity for me. You know how I feel about flying, but I really want this. I need Your help."

Cast all your anxiety on him because he cares for you.

The verse from First Peter rolled over in my mind. Jesus had walked through so many experiences with me before. Why did I think this would be hard for Him?

Why was it so hard for me?

In that moment, I rolled the endless list of questions, worry, and anxiety over on Him. Not that I didn't still have a nervous stomach, but I also had a peace that only God can give.

To my delight, I later learned that one of the other authors would be flying out of the same airport that I was. We'd be catching the same connecting flight. I wouldn't be alone.

As all the notifications from the airlines kept coming, asking if I wanted to pick my seat or pay ahead to check my luggage, I felt peace. I didn't need any of those things. I had an assurance that Jesus was taking care of it all.

The morning I flew out, I met the other author at the airport. While we didn't have seats together on the plane, we were able to spend the time at the airport chatting and getting to know each other. It was especially helpful during the layover. My carry-on never had to be checked. I was assigned a window seat every time. My fellow passengers in my row were a delight to visit with. I even met a couple who had moved to America from England.

Once the retreat was over, my flight home was such that three of us found ourselves with a layover in Houston. I was originally going to be spending several hours there alone, but another lady's flight was delayed. Once again, I had someone with me for most of the journey and layover. After she boarded her flight, I spent a few hours alone in the Houston airport, but I realized I was never really alone. Jesus had walked the whole trip with me as I clung to His Word.

When I cast my cares on Jesus, He took care of every detail. I just had to trust Him. Going to that retreat has been a life-changing experience for me in far greater ways than the writing contract alone. After coming back, I noticed myself stepping out of my comfort zone to do more things I would have been too anxious to try before. It's as if winning the victory to take that flight by casting my anxiety on the Lord showed me what great things can happen when I let Him have my fears.

Faith Step
When anxiety rises up with all its questions and what-ifs, stop to take a quiet moment with Jesus. Cast all your fears and anxiety on Him.

Nothing Can Separate Us

HEATHER JEPSEN

For I am convinced that neither death nor life, neither angels nor demons, neither the present nor the future, nor any powers, neither height nor depth, nor anything else in all creation, will be able to separate us from the love of God that is in Christ Jesus our Lord.

—Romans 8:38–39, NIV

Nothing that happens to us in life can separate us from God's love. Read that again. Nothing that happens to us in our lives can separate us from God's love. Is there any more reassuring word from scripture?

I am a pastor, and I use this verse most often at funerals. During the time of mourning and grief, this is a reminder to families that even though they are going through what is perhaps the hardest time in their lives, they are still connected to God. And it serves as a reminder to them that the one they love who has passed on is also still connected to God. If death cannot separate us from God's love, then nothing can.

I've been in ministry for twenty years now, and the longer I live my life the more I cling to this scripture for hope. When we are young, we often imagine that life will be easy. We imagine growing up and finding our life's mate, maintaining perfect relationships and families, seeing sunshine every day, experiencing good health and financial stability. But, of course, that is often not how things work out.

When I began my ministry career, my first church was a real challenge. The people there liked to argue, and I don't do well with arguing. There was a lot of tension around the fact that I was a woman, something I couldn't help. And, of course, I had a lot of learning to do too. It was my first call after all, and I admittedly made some mistakes there that I have regretted as I have grown older and learned more.

The interesting thing about that challenging period of my life is that it didn't separate me from God. You might imagine that working in the church and having it be heartbreak would make me angry with the Lord. But instead, it drew me closer to God. I better understood God's capacity for forgiveness. I learned more about God's power to bring together people of all backgrounds and outlooks to form one church. I wondered at the power of God and the capacity for love in community. I marveled at how people with so little could also be so generous. My time of trial and hardship did not separate me from the love of God. It taught me what the love of God is.

The same is true when I struggled through growing my personal family. I have two children whom I love deeply, and they are the result of two difficult pregnancies. I had to give birth to my firstborn via cesarian section. I didn't get the birth experience I imagined. Instead, it was rushing and cutting, painful recovery, and not even being able to lift my newborn. Yet my heart grew threefold. The suffering of giving birth, as many mothers can attest to, only broadens and stretches our hearts for motherhood. No pain in motherhood separates us from God's love. Rather, the pain of motherhood deepens our understanding of what it means to love.

One of the biggest challenges in my ministry career, one of my darkest moments, was the suicide of a young man in our congregation. If anything could separate us from God's love, it would be that. Such a loss, such despair and sadness, such fear and worry and wondering why. Yet as the church filled with mourners for the funeral of this young man, I was not without the love of God. My heart was full of courage and strength. I preached forgiveness and hope, and we left together knowing that we were loved and that God held that young man and his heartbreak. Nothing can separate us from the love of God.

The deepest pain and suffering I have personally felt comes from my own health struggles. I have a rare disease, giant cell tumor, where aggressive tumors grow in the tendon of my left ankle. I have fought the disease for six years, trying various treatments, including surgeries to remove the tumors, chemotherapy to shrink the tumors, and even replacing the tendon with a new tendon. Nothing has worked. Always the tumors return; always I struggle with pain when I walk. Now I am facing an amputation of my left foot and lower leg. It can be hard to find hope in such a future.

Even still, I feel the closeness of God's love. I know that the suffering I experience deepens my faith. Throughout my journey with this painful disease, I have felt myself grow as a person. I can better relate to the suffering of others because I know suffering. And I have less fear for suffering in my future, for I know God is with me when I suffer.

Nothing can separate us from the love of God. In our lives we will suffer. We will experience sickness and loss. We will suffer broken dreams and the hardship of a crushed spirit. We will have hard days. Those hard days, those struggles, those times of grief and sorrow—they do not, they cannot, separate us from God's love. In my own life, I have found that they actually deepen my understanding of God's love.

I don't believe that God allows suffering in order to teach us lessons or make us stronger people. But I do believe that in our suffering we can grow. Throughout my life, my times of suffering have drawn me closer to God. And more than anything, they have helped me to understand God's deep and abiding love for us. God is love. And nothing can separate us from that love. What a reason to give thanks to God.

Faith Step
Take a prayerful moment to think back on the hard times of your life. Where have you seen God's love shining through? Have your times of hardship taught you anything about God's love?

In God's Time

TERRIE TODD

The LORD will accomplish what concerns me.

—Psalm 138:8, NASB

These words above appear on canvas on my home office wall, where I enjoy a clear view from my writing desk. The photo behind the words features a cluster of cranberry blossoms, some of the tiny flowers open and others still buds. I love this image of potential and more beauty still to come. I could have spared myself a lot of pain if I'd embraced this message earlier in life, especially as it pertains to my career as an author.

My writing journey goes back to seventh grade when my English teacher praised my ability to crank out something creative with pen and paper. I didn't think much about writing as a skill until decades later. As a young mother, I'd send out annual Christmas newsletters. I was surprised by how much I enjoyed writing them and how much our friends enjoyed reading them.

When I began a puppet ministry at our church, which later led to drama ministry, I began learning scriptwriting. After my first article for our church newsletter prompted an encouraging note from a member I hadn't met, I began to think maybe this was something I could do.

I began sending scripts to publishers of church dramas. When every attempt resulted in a rejection letter, I felt shattered. I thought, *Who needs this? I can't live with this rejection. Maybe I'm not meant to get published. I cannot put myself through this again. It's too painful.*

Years passed, and as I joined a writers' group and continued to try, I learned that rejection is a big part of writing. Some writers even set goals of so many rejections per day, believing an acceptance would come eventually. I began to understand that rejection wasn't failure unless I failed to learn from it. I began entering contests and submitting things to publishers. I saw the occasional acceptance letter in with the rejections. I won the odd contest. Those small successes gave me the courage to keep going and the confidence to take rejections in stride. I can't honestly say I learned to enjoy rejection letters, but with each one, I could check off another attempt, another risk that I'd dared to take.

I made a deal with God. I would do my part and trust Him to do His. My part was fourfold: to keep writing, to keep learning, to keep submitting my work, and to keep praying over it. Everything else—who published my work and when, who read it, liked it, bought it, reviewed it—remained solely in God's hands. The verse above became my theme when tempted to forget my part or stop trusting God for His.

By the time another ten years passed, my fiftieth birthday approached. The notion of writing a book had surfaced. I started writing a split-time novel because I loved reading them, and I chose the World War II era for the historical part of the story. A contest sponsored by a Winnipeg publisher gave me the motivation and deadline I needed to finish the manuscript for *The Silver Suitcase* and enter it. The winning book would be published.

Months later, when the publisher released its short list and my book did not appear, my journal entry revealed how little I'd learned about accepting rejection:

When, God? I am fifty years old. You might be timeless, but I'm not getting any younger. I thought we had a deal. My job is to write and to put my stuff out there. Your job is to take it from there. I have been working so hard, I feel like my fingers are going to bleed some days. I've submitted enough writing to fill volumes, and meanwhile, You're taking a holiday or something. When will You do Your part? I can't do this anymore. I can't handle the rejection. Maybe I was never cut out to write after all. Who was I kidding?

But God knew neither I nor my book were ready. Meanwhile, the publication of two plays, several short inspirational stories, and a weekly column in our local paper encouraged me to stick with it.

In 2011, I entered a revised version of *The Silver Suitcase* in the Christian Writers Guild's Operation First Novel contest and was floored when it made the top ten. It didn't win, but I attended the conference, made new connections, and learned a lot. I began taking their writing courses.

The next year, I entered again. This time, I made the top five. I didn't win. But I was able to write the following words in my journal:

God loves me too much to let me receive things for which I'm not ready. Too much to allow my book to see publication before it's the best it can be. Too much to make this easy for me. Too much to not teach me patience and persistence. Too much to strike me dead for questioning His strange timing. Too much to let my influence outgrow my character.

The next year, I entered again. I made the top five again. I didn't win. I cried—a lot.

The attention, however, won me my first agent in 2013. Another two years would pass, riddled with rejections, before we found a publisher for *The Silver Suitcase*. I was elated. The book released in 2016 and was quickly followed by two more in 2017. They did well, and I thought I was on my way.

When my publisher discontinued its fiction line, I wasn't too distraught. I figured by now I had a big enough following I could easily find another publisher. I even retired from my day job when I turned sixty in 2019.

Alas, I was a naive sixty-year-old.

Though I would eventually publish more books, I've faced far more rejections and far, far fewer dollars coming in than I did for those first three novels. The industry has changed. My dream of releasing a new book each year with a major Christian publisher seems far beyond my grasp now. I've learned I need to practice what I preach, which is that when God does not grant your heart's desire, it generally means He has something better in store for you.

So I cling to the truth that the Lord will accomplish what concerns me. The words provide a daily, affirming reminder when I receive rejections or less-than-stellar reviews. When I feel overwhelmed or I've been overlooked for some opportunity or I feel the weight of unanswered prayers, they speak deeply to my heart. It's not up to me. Yes, I must do my part and finish the work I'm called to. The rest is for God to accomplish—in His time and His way.

Faith Step

In what area of your life do you need to separate your part from God's part as you pursue your dream? Take some time to identify the tasks that are yours. Commit to them wholeheartedly. Then trust God for the outcome, returning to this commitment and trust every day.

Prayers for Comfort

KATHY HENDLEY

Praise be to the God and Father of our Lord Jesus Christ, the Father of compassion and the God of all comfort, who comforts us in all our troubles, so that we can comfort those in any trouble with the comfort we ourselves receive from God.

—2 Corinthians 1:3–4, NIV

I set up for the Bible study armed with a new program and a gut full of nerves. I'd led other groups, but this new group registration didn't show any participants. To my relief, two ladies entered the room and introduced themselves.

"I can't get past it. I can't," said Debbie, holding back tears. "I close my eyes and see my mom lying in that hospital." She paused and shook her head.

"Was that in 2019?" Jackie asked. "That was a bad year for me." She reached over and patted Debbie on the back. "What do we do about it?" Jackie asked me.

I opened our text and read the following scripture: "Praise be to the God and Father of our Lord Jesus Christ, the Father of compassion and the God of all comfort, who comforts us in all our troubles, so that we can comfort those in any trouble with the comfort we ourselves receive from God" (2 Corinthians 1:3–4, NIV).

Jackie sat back against the couch and slapped her knees. Debbie shook her head. "What do we do with that?"

"I'm gonna write it down." Jackie reached for her notebook.

"Let's pray the words and see what happens." I had nothing else. *How do I help someone hurting so badly?*

Later that evening, when I was walking the dog, Debbie's words echoed in my thoughts: *I can't get past it.* I tried to remember the scripture from our lesson. Something about God and comfort. I muttered a meager prayer about comfort for Debbie, but I left the moment feeling empty and useless.

I brought coffee and donuts for the next meeting. "How are you doing this week, Debbie?" I offered her a donut.

"About the same," she spoke with a smile and selected a glazed donut.

"I've been thinking," said Jackie, pulling out her journal and flipping through it. "What if we memorized this scripture?"

"Memorize it?" Debbie wiggled in her chair, shaking her head. "Girl, I can't even remember to bring a pen. No way I'm gonna remember Bible verses."

I'd done my share of memory work during high school. I thought I would be done at graduation.

I can't get past it. Debbie's words came back to me.

"I'll try it." *Did I say that out loud?*

"What?" Debbie stared at me with her eyes and mouth wide open.

"It's worth a try at least," I spoke softly. My memory wasn't as sharp as it used to be either.

"There was something about that first line, 'Praise be to the God,' that hit me right here." Jackie placed her hand on her chest. "Every time I said it." She closed her eyes and smiled.

"OK, OK! I'll try it, but I'm not making any promises." Debbie held her hands up in surrender.

Over the next few weeks, I endeavored to memorize the verses. Every day, I went out to walk the dog and tried to say them aloud.

"The Father of compassion and the God of all comfort . . . or was it the Father of our Lord Jesus and God of compassion?"

I argued with myself about the exact words. "God of all comfort, who comforts us in all our troubles."

How did I do this before?

I pulled up the scripture in my phone and repeated the first line. "Praise be to the God and Father of our Lord Jesus Christ." I decided to stick with a few words until they stuck in my memory.

When I got back to Bible study, I asked the girls, "How's the memory work?"

"Not bad." Jackie pulled out her notebook. "I think I got the first half of it."

"Debbie?"

"Not even close." She shook her head. "I stopped trying after the first day. But I read it every day."

"Same here. I repeat the first few words when I walk the dog, but I'm not through verse one yet." I grinned.

Throughout the winter, we encouraged one another to memorize the verses. We took a break for the summer. Travel and kids made it difficult for us to meet regularly. When we did come back together, I asked them about the verses.

"Is it getting any better?" I'd already opened to the scripture in my Bible.

"Not yet." Debbie forced a smile.

I sat a little taller because I'd been able to get to the next verse, "who comforts us in all our troubles."

Jackie spoke up, "I got up to verse six. I'm not sure how far we wanted to go with it."

She took the wind out of my sails, but I took a deep breath. "I say you go as far you can. I'm stuck on 'comforts us in all our troubles.'"

"That part still makes me cry." Debbie fumbled through her bag for a tissue. "I don't know why it's still so hard for me."

We gathered around for a group hug. I needed God to comfort her because I didn't quite understand her grief either. I tried to relate.

"Troubles come in many different forms," I said as I patted her on the back.

Groups come and go. Our work schedules changed again. I saw Debbie and Jackie at church, but we weren't able to meet as before. Debbie kept us all in the loop with frequent texts and cards. I saw the life return to her. She had received comfort from God.

My day of sorrow came a couple of years later. As Debbie described, I remember the day my dad passed away. In the midst of my sorrow, I texted Debbie, and she responded quickly, "Praying for you, sweet lady."

A few days later, unable to handle any more condolences, I took the dog for a walk. My mind went blank. I couldn't do memory work today. I couldn't do thinking work either. A phrase crept into my head: "who comforts us in all our troubles."

The words floated from the depths of my memory, and a great weight lifted from my shoulders. Comfort. For the first time in days, I walked in comfort and unmistakable peace.

Debbie met me at the funeral. She had taken time off work to be with me. "I understand what it means now," she said with a smile. "I went through all of that to help you right now." She gave me a big hug.

Comfort. I felt it again as if it had been the first time. Grief comes in waves, but so does comfort.

"Thank you for coming. I know this must be hard for you."

Debbie smiled and said, "I know how hard this is for you, and I wouldn't miss it for the world."

Faith Step

Memorizing scripture can be challenging, but it can also offer comfort when we least expect it. Choose a particular verse or verses that speak to you. Take each verse one word or phrase at a time. Repetition helps! Try writing it in a journal or notebook, and then try saying it aloud.

Redefining My Identity

AMY CATLIN WOZNIAK

Therefore I tell you, her sins, which are many, are forgiven—for she loved much. But he who is forgiven little, loves little.

—Luke 7:47, ESV

When I was five years old, my father became terminally ill and passed away. Many of my memories in the years after his death are blurry. But I do remember sitting atop the monkey bars in second grade when a boy's voice cut through the playground noise: "She's the girl without a daddy." I looked down, and he was pointing right at me. Something in his tone made it feel as though my father's absence was my fault. I scrambled down the metal rungs and ran to the far end of the playground, pressing my face against the brick school building, hoping no one would see my tears.

"Girl without a daddy" was just the first of many labels I've worn. Even after I became a believer, I allowed labels like *fatherless*, *divorcée*, and *not enough* to shape how I saw myself. They clung to me like those orange clearance stickers slapped on things no one wanted—branding me as unworthy, diminishing my value, and making me question if even God's love could reach me.

That shame held me captive, whispering, "You did that. How can you even look at yourself, let alone have God see you?" And this shame was keeping me from becoming the woman God created me to be; I couldn't believe I had a purpose in God's Kingdom.

In July 2014, my stepson Ryan was killed in a tragic accident. The weight of the grief hit me like a wave I couldn't escape.

I went to church, but I was angry with God. I turned inward—pushing away everyone who tried to help. I was drowning in my grief and swimming further away from everyone and everything I loved.

After months of silence, and desperate to find a way out of the numbness, I picked up my laptop and began to type. The words came slowly at first, but soon, the anger, the grief, the memories I had buried deep inside spilled out onto the screen, helping to still the chaos rolling through me. Over time, those journal pages became a letter to God, and writing became my way of talking to Him again.

Even still, I could feel Him nudging me to go deeper. It was time to open the vaults of my heart where I shoved my hidden shame, sin, and regrets. But healing those locked places would require God's hand in the deep, dark corners of my soul.

As He peeled away the layers—starting with my deep grief—I began to rediscover pieces of myself. With every layer, I heard the echoes of the little girl I had silenced for so long. My need to be strong had kept her quiet, but now, bit by bit, fragments of long-lost memories surfaced, and I began reclaiming parts of myself I thought were gone forever.

As I retraced the steps on my journey, I discovered the passage of time had shown God to be faithful in replacing those scorched places of ruin with divine beauty, revealing the bigger picture of who He was calling me to be. During that time, I accepted an invitation to co-lead an online Bible study with my friend Debbie. I was excited at first, but as the start date approached, fear crept in.

Who am I to do this? I wondered. *How can I lead others when my own story is tangled with mistakes?*

A spiritual mentor shared how certain verses had helped her along the way. One of them was Luke 7:47 (ESV): "Her sins, which are many, are forgiven—for she loved much." Here was someone I admired, who had also carried the weight of her sins—yet she had found peace. I began clinging to that verse even as doubts assailed me with whispered reminders of my failures.

Slowly, the meaning of the verse sank in. Jesus's forgiveness doesn't stop at the surface—it reaches deep, peeling away every label shame had slapped on me. His opinion was the only one that mattered. And in His eyes, my sins—although many—were forgiven, just like the woman who wept at His feet and wiped them with her hair.

Along the way, I found someone on Etsy who makes personalized bracelets. I ordered one with Luke 7:47 on the front and "Her sins, which are many, are forgiven" on the back. It became something tangible I could hold on to when old labels resurfaced or when new shame threatened to pull me back.

Every time I feel the bracelet against my wrist, I remember that those labels no longer define me. My true identity is in Christ. Jesus has given me a clean slate, and the only label I need to wear is daughter of the King.

Seven years have passed since Debbie and I started that Bible study, and it's still going strong. We've gathered women from all backgrounds into a safe space where we study God's Word and shed the labels that once defined us. Together, we embrace the truth that God is bigger than our shame, our failures, and our doubts.

It didn't happen all at once, but over time, God began sculpting the jagged pieces of my heart back together and made me whole again. From those ashes, He gave me healing I can't explain and the promise of a future reunion with those I've lost.

The truth is we all carry shame—wounds we'd rather hide than confront. Maybe it's a financial mistake, a broken relationship, or an addiction. Those labels can keep us from living the abundant and purpose-filled life God intends.

But we don't have to carry them. I still wear that bracelet with Luke 7:47 inscribed on it to remind me that all my sins are forgiven.

You are not your past, and you are not your mistakes. The first step toward healing is inviting Him to reach into the deepest, most broken places of your heart and then letting Jesus peel away the labels that no longer serve you, transforming you from the inside out and offering the clean slate He went to the cross to provide.

If you let Him, His truth will replace every lie—every label—you've believed because you are a fully known, fully loved, and deeply cherished beloved child of God.

Faith Step

Reflect on any labels of shame you've been carrying—whether placed on you by others or by yourself. Ask Jesus to peel away those labels and reveal the truth of your identity in Him. Then choose a Bible verse to remind you of this truth, and place it somewhere visible in your life as a daily reminder.

Remain in Me

EMILY C. MARSZALEK

"Remain in me, and I will remain in you. For a branch cannot produce fruit if it is severed from the vine, and you cannot be fruitful unless you remain in me."

—John 15:4, NLT

Examining in the mirror my cross tattoo with "Christ is King" written inside, I felt my heart sink. It was a tattoo I had proudly acquired at eighteen, stationed in the center of my back just below the neckline—a visual reminder of my faith and commitment to Christ as King and Lord of my life. But Christ had not been my King or Lord for many years. A tattoo I once treasured as a token of my faith had morphed into a painful reminder of just how far I had strayed.

As I was growing up in a Christian household, my parents demonstrated what it looked like to love and follow Jesus and taught me and my brothers to do the same. We faithfully attended church, enjoyed healthy prayer lives, regularly relished fellowship with other believers, blasted praise and worship music in the home, and established Bible reading as a practice as habitual as brushing our teeth.

Even at a young age, I fostered a ravenous hunger for the Bible. Throughout high school, after my homework was completed, I lay in my bunkbed and studied my Bible for hours, reading it cover to cover several times over. The more scripture I consumed, the more I hungered for it. Soon enough, reading scripture wasn't enough; I wanted the Word written on my heart. I began memorizing scriptures using flash cards. My stack of memorized verses continued to expand through these early years, growing several inches thick. I prioritized God and remained in Him. As a result, He remained in me. I maintained peace, joy, and excitement for what God had in store for my life.

In my early twenties, however, a shift occurred. It began gradually. Attending university, I was exceedingly busy with academic studies and extracurriculars. Time was always in short supply, and my priorities altered to accommodate. Instead of waking early to spend time reading the Bible as I had done for many years, I wanted that extra twenty minutes of sleep. Rather than spending quiet time in prayer to center myself on Christ before I jetted off into the day, I craved a scroll through my Facebook feed. Instead of attending church on Sunday mornings, I wanted to avoid setting an alarm and savor a commitment-free morning. Time with God continued to fall lower and lower on my to-do list until it disappeared altogether.

What began as a slow and steady shift had in time become momentous. My prayer life perished, I no longer attended church, friendships with other Christians fizzled, and my beloved Bible became nothing more than an expert dust collector. The consequences on my life were equally momentous. Where I was previously filled with Christ, a void developed. Into that void came confusion, hopelessness, and sin. The firm foundation I had built my life on had crumbled by my own neglect. I was no longer the joyful, peace-filled, and loving person I once was. Rather, I was stricken with anxiety, confusion, and even anger.

In a futile attempt to regain the peace and joy I once savored, I sought joy and fulfillment in all the wrong places—unhealthy relationships, substances, social media accolades, and achievement to name a few. As I was increasingly filled with worldly things, however, the void within me grew deeper and darker. I felt empty and began to view life as meaningless. Despite having a seemingly successful and fulfilling life, hopelessness peppered my every day.

Reflecting on my childhood and teen years in which I was filled with the love, peace, and hope I so longed for now, I questioned what had changed. I still had a wonderful and supportive family, a job that met my needs, and even a healthy relationship with a good man whom I would later marry. One area of my life, however, had drastically changed—my devotion to my faith. I still identified as a Christian and believed in Jesus, but He had not been the Lord of my life for many years.

I recognized my need to return to Christ in repentance, but a question haunted me. *How had I strayed so far?* There was no single event or radical change that made me reject the faith or turn from my walk with Christ. Rather, it was a gradual shift that over time became immense and life-altering. I feared that such drifting would happen again.

Continuing to ponder this question, I began reincorporating daily devotions back into my mornings. In one such devotion, Jesus's words in John 15 were highlighted. When I read John 15:4, I was dumbstruck. Jesus's words held the answer to my question: "Remain in me, and I will remain in you. For a branch cannot produce fruit if it is severed from the vine, and you cannot be fruitful unless you remain in me." This was the key.

Christ didn't remain in me during those difficult years because I didn't remain in Him. As I no longer invested in my relationship with Him through prayer, worship, Bible reading, and fellowship with other believers, I was increasingly filled with worldly things that offered only fleeting joy, peace, and fulfillment before leaving me even emptier than before.

As I read and reread John 15:4, my eyes were opened to a simple yet profound truth: only when I remain in Him will He remain in me, and only when He remains in me will my life produce the fruitfulness I seek. As I recognized what I had allowed to occur, with an open and humble heart, I reaffirmed both my repentance and devotion to God.

My actions and priorities have mirrored this renewed devotion. I've returned to God's Word with the same ravenous hunger I once fostered as a child. The more I learn, the more I crave to learn more. I've devoured books on Christian theology and have sought out additional Bible studies online. I listen to Christian radio while I get ready for work each morning, ensuring that I begin each day with a heart of worship. I talk to God throughout the day, sharing my successes and failures. I've begun not only faithfully attending church each week but also serving in the church, enjoying fellowship with other believers.

I've even resurrected my old stack of Bible verse flash cards to aid in scripture memorization. John 15:4 was one of the first scriptures I added to the ever-growing stack. Jesus's words in this verse continue to act as a daily reminder that as I am increasingly filled with Him, my life produces great fruitfulness and He satisfies and quenches my thirsty soul. As I remain in Him, He will remain in me. It's as simple as that.

Now, each morning as I observe my cross tattoo in the mirror, I am reminded that only when I remain in Christ am I truly satisfied, filled, and able to experience the life-altering love and peace that I so long for.

Faith Step

Prioritize and invest in your relationship with Christ through study of scripture, prayer, worship, and fellowship with other believers.

Stumbling but Not Falling

CHELSEA OHLEMILLER

God is within her, she will not fall; God will help her at break of day.

—Psalm 46:5, NIV

Life has buried me under loss, defeat, and uncertainty more times than I can count. I've lost out on opportunities. I've been heartbroken from love and relationships. I've been devastated by profound grief and mourning. I've watched darkness overshadow the radiant light, feeling how trauma can deceive us into believing our faith is fragile and unstable. I've seen hope fade in myself and in others.

Each experience, drenched in unfortunate circumstances, slowly chipped away at my confidence, leaving me questioning my worth and the path I thought I knew so well. Failure whispers its own sentiments that can reshape my perspective on strength, resilience, and faith.

Staring at the stack of rejection letters on my desk and in my inbox felt like evidence of failure. Stepping on the scale in the bathroom and seeing the numbers increase—rather than decrease—felt like failure. Lying on the doctor's examination table, unable to hold and keep a healthy pregnancy and child, felt like failure of the most extreme kind. Watching my mother die from a disease that no doctor or I could save her from felt like failure, harsh and heartbreaking failure.

Failure is a complex force—relentless and unforgiving, it carves deep wounds of doubt, paralyzes with fear, and dismantles the very trust you once held in yourself and the world.

After losing my mother and her invaluable guidance, I found myself desperately searching for inspiration to navigate my darkest times, those laced with mistakes and frustration. In this quest, I continually encountered this powerful verse on social media: "God is within her, she will not fail."

Yet there I was—failing.

I've had many failures in my life, scattered all the way from youth to adulthood. Failure is, in fact, a reality of life. So why did this Psalmist's verse say I wouldn't fail? If God can proclaim such a bold promise, why had I not been privy to it?

One night in sorrow and desperation, I pulled out my Bible, a little dustier than I'd like to admit but ready for me, welcoming the intention and attention. I opened to the verse that had me so bewildered. The one that had me feeling forgotten and unworthy. The one that had me believing I was a failure.

Psalm 46:5 (NIV) read, "God is within her, she will not fall: God will help her at break of day." I read the words slowly and with purpose—and then noticed a beautiful distinction in its message. The Word of God says *fall* not *fail*, a very delicate but powerful difference. I read the words again and again to be sure I hadn't read incorrectly.

I made no mistake. The scripture distinctly says *fall*.

This verse doesn't promise that we won't fail but that we will not fall. That tiny distinction changed everything for me. It taught me that with God, I may stumble, but I'll never be defeated. He is our strength and our help. He is on our side, in all seasons, even the seasons of darkness and failure. His work is not done. We are not done.

Failure is not an ending. It is an opportunity for transformation and trust.

Our strength might be shakable, but God's is not. If we get knocked down from life's burdens and destruction, we will prevail through Him. We will rise again with His help. This revelation from scripture reignited my hope. Yes, there will be challenges. There will be hard times. There will be difficulties, and we will stumble. But no challenge, no experience, no obstacle is insurmountable with God's strength and promises.

This isn't an individual journey. He is with us, always. He is the grit that finds us when we're about to give up. He is the effort and the courage to try again when our lives have been filled with "No" and "Better luck next time." He is the strength to keep persisting and the encouragement that reminds us to keep dreaming and setting goals as high as the moon and the stars. We are made in His plan, imperfect but never failures.

After a moment of breathing in the beauty of scripture's distinctions and letting go of my misunderstanding of this verse, I read the remaining line: "God will help her at break of day." And I remember what I've learned in the pews of church about that phrase "break of day." The beauty of His promise is not that there will not be darkness or harsh times but rather that the sun will rise. The light will shine again. Something incredible will burst from the darkness with His glory and His guidance.

Often our worldly failures aren't failures at all but rather God's redirection. God's way of bringing us closer to His refuge and further from the chaos and instability of our world. Further from the things we wanted but didn't need. Further from the things we envisioned in our lives but that were never part of His plan. Failure is simply a tool for growth and transformation, not something tied to our worth, our purpose, or our capabilities.

Gripping my Bible through tears, I was overwhelmed by the truth I'd just encountered. Determined not to forget the power of this message, I carefully jotted down Psalm 46:5 on a note card and tucked it into my planner—a reminder for the next time I faced life's challenges or stumbled along the way. More importantly, it was a reminder to seek God's Word in its purest form, rather than relying on the versions that flood social media with trendy graphics.

I long to be guided by truth, allowing life's experiences to draw me closer to God rather than pull me away due to misunderstandings or misrepresentations of His Word. The true message of God was always there, written perfectly, waiting for me to read it.

Failure may bruise us, but with God, it will never break us. His promise was never that we wouldn't stumble but that we would never be lost to the fall. In His strength, we find the courage to rise again, knowing that no setback can overshadow His unfailing grace.

Faith Step
When you see a Bible verse quote on social media, go to your Bible to see the verse in context and to soak in what that verse means for your life.

Surrender in Suffering

BECKY HOFSTAD

> Not only so, but we also glory in our sufferings, because we know that suffering produces perseverance; perseverance, character; and character, hope. And hope does not put us to shame, because God's love has been poured out into our hearts through the Holy Spirit, who has been given to us.
>
> —Romans 5:3–5, NIV

I looked up at the imposing maple tree in the center of our backyard and thought about our stalled adoption process. Ten feet above the ground, the tree divided into three long fingers that reached for the sky as if pointing me to Heaven. Half of the yellowed leaves above my head were intact. They refused to yield to the rhythm of the seasons. They may not fall before a heavy snowfall comes and bows the branches.

God, will our new daughter see snow for the first time this winter? I inquired in silence.

As I raked crinkly leaves into piles, the carpet of dull green grass under my feet grew larger with each stroke. My heart rate rose as my muscles tensed and my lungs filled with the earthy smell of early November air. Getting the leaves off the lawn felt like progress.

If only hard work could bring Naomi to us. She was half a world away. She had legally become our daughter on September 13 of that year when a judge in Liberia, Africa, signed the court decree. That, however, wasn't the last hurdle before we could travel to her, before we could bring her to our home. With each exhalation, I longed for the worry over the delays to dislodge from deep inside, but my mind would not rest.

On paper my husband and I were new parents, but we'd never met our daughter. Our primary connection to her consisted of sending a few care packages containing clothes and toys. The last one included a raincoat with Hello Kitty on the front pocket for the rainy season. We had arranged four photos of Naomi on our kitchen table like a shrine. Each day as we sat at the table, we basked in her two-dimensional grin. We wondered what lay behind the twinkle in her brown eyes. Was there a mischievous streak in our five-year-old?

In the three years we'd spent in the process, I often wondered how someone without faith endured the ups and downs, the uncertainty, and the miles of separation inherent to international adoption. "With God everything is possible" (Matthew 19:26, NLT) was a promise that encouraged us, especially when we were thinking about the urgency of our situation.

Naomi had health issues. Her head was enlarged, and she'd never walked. Hydrocephalus, excess cerebral spinal fluid in the ventricles of her brain, was suspected. Because she didn't have access to an MRI, we had no definite diagnosis—and we wouldn't until she came to the United States. Would her health remain stable until we could bring her home? Would she be able to walk one day? We hoped that God would make it possible through a medical device surgically installed in Naomi's brain, through physical therapy, and through the power of His healing.

On the more difficult days, I wrestled with verses like this one: "Not only so, but we also glory in our sufferings, because we know that suffering produces perseverance" (Romans 5:3, NIV). The perseverance piece resonated with me. Growing up on a farm, I was no stranger to sticking to a job until it was finished. But what would it look like for me to glory in this suffering? To rejoice because no one in Liberia could determine whether to put Naomi's current last name or her new last name on her passport? Celebrate because without a passport, no visa to travel to the United States could be issued? Exalt in the fact that without these documents our travel to Africa to complete our daughter's adoption was not possible?

As I scooped up an armful of leaves to fill the next bag, I wished someone would scoop me up. My soul felt buried, as if I were under a pile of leaves. I wanted to be able to do something—anything—to move things along in our adoption process. So much of my suffering stemmed from my lack of control over the situation. At my worst moments, I refused to trust God. I wanted to be the one in control.

I put my rake down, looked up at the sky, and asked, *God, when are You going to act?*

Almost before the whispered question left my lips, my throat constricted. Should I be talking to God this way? Throughout my life, I'd seen His perfect timing in other circumstances. Just as I knew the snow would come, I knew that the paperwork logjam would eventually break. The current state of paralysis brought on by a change in how birth certificates were issued in Liberia couldn't last forever. I knew the new measures had been put in place to prevent human trafficking. Surely, I could be encouraged in knowing children would be better protected.

Yet I also believed that for some reason this delay was in God's timing. I knew He would use it to bring about His purposes. I also knew the maple trees would eventually surrender their leaves, even if they fell on top of snow. I knew I needed to surrender my desire to be in control. I needed to trust God.

Only one small strip of lawn remained to be cleared of leaves. As the sun faded, I wanted to go inside and drink some hot chocolate to chase away the chill that was settling in but decided this was one task I could finish. As I raked, I thought about the model of the verse in Romans: "suffering produces perseverance; perseverance, character; and character, hope (Romans 5:3–4, NIV).

As I put my rake away, I was grateful that despite the delays, my heart was filled with anticipation. Naomi was our daughter. God had called us to adopt her. Over the months and over the miles, my husband and I had grown to love her. I focused my mind on what I knew was true: God dearly loved us and dearly loved Naomi. That thought enabled me to press on, with hope.

A week later, we received news that Naomi's adoption could move forward with a passport issued in her birth name. We traveled three days later and have been blessed to bask in Naomi's three-dimensional grin for over ten years. God has made it possible for her to walk, jump, and even ski down snow-covered hills.

When I look back on that time of waiting, I see that it drew me closer to God. God doesn't cause our suffering, and we won't see beyond it until we get to that stage. When we're ready, embracing the cycle of perseverance, character, and hope strengthens our faith. We surrender to God, putting our full trust in His timing and His ways. For as we read in the letter to the Romans, "Hope does not put us to shame, because God's love has been poured out into our hearts through the Holy Spirit, who has been given to us" (5:5, NIV).

Faith Step

Identify a time in your life when you were suffering. Looking back, how did you persevere? How did that time build your character? Your hope in God? How can you surrender any current trials to God by embracing the perseverance, character, hope model of Romans 5:3–5? What would it look like for you to glory or rejoice in your suffering?

The Beauty and Power of Lament

JANET LAIRD MULLEN

How long, LORD? Will you forget me forever? How long will you hide your face from me? How long must I wrestle with my thoughts and day after day have sorrow in my heart? How long will my enemy triumph over me? Look on me and answer, LORD my God. Give light to my eyes, or I will sleep in death, and my enemy will say, "I have overcome him," and my foes will rejoice when I fall. But I trust in your unfailing love; my heart rejoices in your salvation. I will sing the LORD's praise, for he has been good to me.

—Psalm 13, NIV

I was only six weeks away from what could be a nasty public trial. Twenty-four months of a protracted divorce had left me mentally, emotionally, and physically exhausted and rather jaded with the legal system. I worried about whether my money would hold out to get through an expensive trial and what it would mean for family relationships as relatives were called to testify. I took a break from my legal concerns to go to my favorite place, the Chapel of Memories, to study in solitude the current session in my Psalms Bible study. This week was focused on Psalms of Lament. I had never studied the Psalms by category and was intrigued to learn that the laments make up the largest grouping.

As I thought about my own family and faith tradition, I realized that lament has always been discouraged. When I was a child, my father would chastise me if he saw tears in my eyes. He would say, "No, don't you dare cry." And compliant child that I was, I obeyed. I swallowed down the tears. I learned that it is unacceptable to express anger or sorrow. It means there is something wrong with me. That I am weak. I imitated my father and diligently never showed disappointment or sadness. I practiced his example so consistently that I earned the right to wear the T-shirt that boasted, "Keep Calm and Carry On." I thought this was a good thing. And I was praised by those around me for always holding it together. It is what people came to expect from me.

My mother also reinforced this message throughout my life, often correcting me if I voiced a complaint or a criticism. She found it unacceptable to complain or criticize about anything. She insisted that I maintain a positive outlook at all times. I leaned into my home and church training, and throughout the months of my disintegrating marriage and the early months of my divorce, I tried to look for the silver lining, to keep my chin up, to soldier on. All the platitudes. I even prided myself on it.

But it was unsustainable.

I understand the value of passing over an offense or avoiding having a critical spirit, but now I also realize that can be taken too far—to the detriment of my own physical, emotional, and spiritual well-being.

Every time I visited my mom at her home and expressed my frustration with the lack of progress with the divorce, she would correct me with a scripture or remind me to trust God. I knew she meant well, but her silencing of my legitimate pain and anger left me feeling hurt and unsupported. I cherish scripture, but I would have to skim over and make a cursory reply to her early morning texts reminding me to trust in Jesus and have faith. I believed I was doing that with every breath I took, and I could not understand why she seemed incapable of understanding how my complaints were not evidence of a lack of trust. And then I met the Psalms of Lament.

There was a scripture I read that June afternoon in the Chapel of Memories as I contemplated going to trial, and it helped me understand that complaint and faith are not incompatible—that, in fact, honesty before God is required for true relationship.

> How long, LORD? Will you forget me forever? How long will you hide your face from me? How long must I wrestle with my thoughts and day after day have sorrow in my heart? How long will my enemy triumph over me? Look on me and answer, LORD my God. Give light to my eyes, or I will sleep in death, and my enemy will say, "I have overcome him," and my foes will rejoice when I fall. (Psalm 13:1–4, NIV)

I immediately identified with the Psalmist's frustration and confusion, and I got on my knees and offered his words on my own behalf. I, too, felt forgotten. I, too, needed to see God's face and experience His deliverance. I felt as if my fate lay in the hands of a human judge—one who knew less about my trouble than any of my family or my friends or my lawyer, yet she would make the final judgment. Trial felt daunting, and waves of nausea swept over me as I thought about it. That afternoon I told the Lord about all my worries. Then I cried. I finally just let the tears stream down. And I sat in silence and faced the fearful depth of the predicament I was in and my helplessness. I asked God, "Why?" And then I waited in silence.

There was no audible voice that answered. But as I rose from my knees, my face and shirt wet with tears, I felt an unmistakable certainty in my heart that I would experience justice. This Psalm of Lament had reminded me of who is the True Judge in my life, and He is both fair and merciful. He knows me. He knows my troubles. And I knew I could walk boldly into whatever lay before me because I had laid my heart bare before my Savior, and He had filled it with Himself.

I've found that being completely honest and vulnerable, even in church—maybe especially in church—can be hard. Despite the prominence of the Psalms of Lament in our Holy Book (many penned by the man after God's own heart), many Christians are uncomfortable with the healthy and necessary process of sorrowing. Just as I was. Some view it as a sign of lack of faith.

But nothing could be further from the truth. Lament brings us close to the heart of our Father who made us and understands us. He knows how we feel. He can empathize. He longs to meet us in our sorrow. Laying our hurts before Him is an act of faith and puts us in a position to receive what our hearts truly need—His authentic love and care in the midst of our circumstances.

That June day, I left the chapel facing the same circumstances that had weighed so heavily on me when I entered. My circumstances had not changed, but I had. Lament had changed me. I knew my God knew what I was facing. And I now carried the certainty that He would see me through those circumstances. And He did.

Faith Step

The next time you find yourself struggling, take a moment to stop what you are doing and find a quiet place. Read Psalm 13 or another of the Psalms of Lament. Then honestly pour out your complaints and sorrows to God. Next, sit quietly and listen for the Spirit to speak into your soul. What is He saying to you? Use the Notes app on your smartphone or a small notebook to record what you heard so that you can read it again later. Then commit to trusting Him. Ask Him to help you. And then just take the next step that He directs. One step. One prayer. He will show you.

The Lord Will Fight for You

MEGAN CONNER

"The LORD will fight for you; you need only to be still."

—Exodus 14:14, NIV

I stared at the bright white walls tinted with yellow as the fluorescent lights illuminated the room around me. I sat quietly next to my twelve-year-old daughter, who, once again, was carrying herself with a strength and peace beyond her years. Addy had just finished her first set of follow-up MRI screens at the hospital, and we were waiting for her neurosurgeon to come in and share the results.

It had been a mere four and a half months since Addy was unexpectedly hospitalized after undiagnosable, crippling back pain and the emergence of paralysis from her waist down. During our previous sojourn at this establishment, Addy endured what felt like unending tests and countless hypotheses until an international team of neurosurgeons concluded she had an extremely rare cyst embedded in the interior of her spinal column that was crushing her spinal cord. The only possible treatment was a risky but necessary operation to attack the assailant. After post-op recovery and relearning how to walk, Addy was released home until today's follow-up appointment.

We were confident this required exam was just a routine visit (or at least we had strongly convinced ourselves of that). The increased anxiety over the past few days and the many tears shed last night and in between screenings and appointments today showed there were obviously a few cracks in our armor. But as I prepared for the day, I prayed, *Lord, whatever is before us, I ask that You give us peace and strength. No matter what happens, You will be with us and You will guide us through. I trust in You.*

Suddenly, our neurosurgeon entered the room. He began a series of neurological tests to ensure Addy hadn't lost any of her movement, sensation, or abilities. All went well. No surprises there since she had been extremely active since her recovery, showing zero signs of her former issues. Then her doctor turned to the computer and said, "OK, let's take a look at your screens."

As soon as the image emerged, I froze. Right there, in the middle, was a horrible white mass. Then he displayed three side-by-side frames.

"You see this first image?" he asked. "This is her screen before surgery. We can see here how the cyst had completely engulfed her spinal column. You can't even see her spinal cord. Now, this next image, the middle one, is the MRI we took a few hours after surgery. You see here how the white area is completely deflated. Her spinal cord is plump and clearly present. We expected this result, and it looked great. Now, this third screen shows her MRI from today."

Immediately, my heart started to pound. I felt sick to my stomach.

"As you can see, the cyst has regrown. You will also notice how the spinal cord has once again taken on a curved, compressed shape, as it is being affected by the reemergence of the cyst."

Tears filled my eyes. I blinked them back rapidly. I had to be strong. Addy sat rigidly erect, taut with tension. The doctor continued to provide explanations for this shocking revelation, all of which were estimations, to say the least. While his comments provided possible justifications, they were a reminder of the phrase "practicing medicine." Addy's case had been unprecedented from the start. Despite all the logical arguments that long-term success could not be guaranteed, it did seem incredibly possible after the surgery. I could not help but feel devastated.

It had not even been five full months, and the cyst had grown to at least half the size it was when she was hospitalized. Its luminous mass glared at us with such intensity we had to almost squint to see what remained visible of her spinal cord. I silently prayed to myself again, *Lord, I prayed this morning that whatever came, You would stay by our side. I trust in You, Lord. Give me wisdom and peace. Grant me the ability to comfort my daughter. Help us all cling to You.*

Addy was just shy of thirteen years old. My biggest concern at thirteen was balancing sports, friends, and homework—not facing possible paralysis (again). There should be a great deal of life ahead of her, God willing. Instead of looking ahead to the dream of what those future years could hold, as so many young people are free to do, here she was facing a future with a bomb trapped inside her body, pressing against her spinal cord, which at any moment could choose to decide its time was up.

I had no answers to quell Addy's fears or assure her that she would not have to endure any more suffering. I only held her while she cried and told her through my own tears we would be OK because God was with us. Somehow, He would see us through it all. He carried us through the last trial, and He would remain with us through whatever else was ahead.

I knew at that moment what the Israelites must have felt facing the Red Sea and with an Egyptian army barreling toward them. Fear and anxiety overwhelmed my mind and heart. I longed for control of anything. I am sure the ancient Israelites felt exactly the same. However, God did not call them to frenzied panic. Instead, He reminded them through Moses, "The LORD will fight for you; you need only to be still."

God had demonstrated His miraculous provision through the plagues and the Israelites' recent exodus. You would think their latest victories would have emboldened courage. Yet we humans are fickle and quickly forget the provision and might of our God. As soon as a new adversity arises, we shudder with fear. Then we immediately strategize, worry, strain, and fight for our own deliverance. But the truth is we are almost always powerless to control our outcomes.

I could not grant my own liberation or offer salvation to my daughter. I would love to say that all was well and she did not endure further hardship. However, we did not receive our desired outcome. Addy ended up back in the hospital just months later and underwent an even more invasive operation the second time around. Thankfully, she appears in remission for now, but there are no assurances of when the unwelcome adversary could possibly arise again. It has taken us all a great deal of surrender, prayer, and faithfulness to learn how to remain at rest and rely on the one true Source of deliverance. The Lord will fight for us. We need only to be still.

Faith Step

One of the most effective tools when battling for faith over fear is declaring the promises of God. Take some time to write down scriptural truths that help you recall God's all-powerful provision for His children. Read and recite these reminders over yourself daily and when you feel the tug of despair. He will fight for you. You need only to be still.

An Open Door

BETH GOOCH

This is the message from the one who is holy and true, the one who has the key of David. What he opens, no one can close; and what he closes, no one can open.

—Revelation 3:7, NLT

My stomach churned as I drove home from the job interview at a local university. They needed a digital producer, the same work I'd done at a newspaper before being laid off. I hadn't received an offer yet, but conversations with my potential boss and coworkers made it clear the work was within my scope. I should've been pleased, but unease washed over me.

Why was my job search so nerve-racking?

A couple of weeks later, I bought a black suit for an interview with a downtown bank. The selection process had narrowed to one other candidate and me. I sat at a long, polished conference table with my prospective boss plus her team of well-dressed marketing specialists. Their friendly questions encouraged me. When the interview ended, my high heels pinched my toes as I walked to my car and tossed the expensive blazer in the back seat.

An hour-long drive home provided plenty of time to think about wearing suits and making that commute. My shoulders tensed. If offered the job, I'd be a fool to turn it down.

But could I fit in?

For years, when I was working in a scruffy newsroom, my uniform was blue jeans and tennis shoes. I tried to imagine sitting primly at a desk on the university campus or at the bank. The idea gave me the heebie-jeebies.

The day after the bank interview, my friend Paula called to check on my progress.

"I'm so confused," I said. "What if I accept a position at the university or bank and hate it? I'd be embarrassed to start and then quit."

"If they offer you a job at that bank or university, go for it. I've been praying a scripture for you. Revelation 3:7." She paraphrased the verse. "What the Lord opens, no one can shut; what He shuts no one can open."

I swallowed. "So you're saying if I apply for a job that's wrong for me, God will close that door?"

"Correct. You can go to any interview with confidence," she said. "If it's the job God wants you to have, He'll open the door. If it's not, He'll slam that door shut."

I thanked Paula before we ended our call and expressed my gratitude to the Lord for a friend who prays and shares scripture.

Kneeling on the bedroom floor, I said, "Lord, I don't want to waste months or even years in a job that is not Your will for me. You promised that what You seal, no one can open. And what You open, no one can seal. I'm asking You to close the doors to any jobs that are wrong for me. If I apply for a position that's not right, I am trusting You to shut that door."

Relief washed over me. No more fretting over those fancy office jobs. If that's where the Lord wanted me to be, He'd equip me to do it. And if He had something else in mind for me, the path would open.

A couple of weeks passed, and I didn't hear from the university or the bank. Oh well. I also applied for several jobs related to my education and work experience at advertising agencies and marketing firms. Some seemed so closely aligned to my skills, and I figured the offers were sure to pour in. But they didn't.

I kept praying Revelation 3:7 and grew bolder.

For years, I'd dreamed of working at a nursery, so I applied at one of the big-box hardware stores, imagining myself working in the garden department. The idea of a job where I'd be up moving around instead of sitting at a desk sounded fun. They never called, though.

An ad for a pharmaceutical fulfillment facility stated a need for someone to count pills and type prescription labels. I applied. Never heard from them.

My friend April said the gym where she led fitness classes needed a childcare worker to mind youngsters while their parents exercised. Childcare? Me? "Does it include a free gym membership?" The answer was yes, so I filled out an application. They hired someone else.

My husband ordered a mechanical item for my car, so I offered to pick it up. When I arrived at the dealership parts department, my former classmate Terry was standing behind the counter.

"Sorry to hear about you losing your job," he said. "You worked at the newspaper your whole life, didn't you?"

"Since I was twenty."

Terry stepped away to retrieve the part, and a stack of job applications on the counter caught my eye. I visualized myself wearing a red polo shirt with the company emblem like Terry's while ringing up purchases for customers.

He returned to the counter.

"Is it OK if I fill out a job application?"

"Sure," he said. But I never got a call.

I sought all kinds of positions and felt no stress about the outcomes. I believed God would close the doors to jobs that were wrong for me, and when the right position came along, He'd swing the door wide open.

Then one day, I got a call.

"I heard you were looking for a job," said Ellen, the director of the women's ministry at my church. She offered me a position that I didn't even know existed—helping write newsletters, emails, and advertising copy, and managing social media accounts. Part of the time, I also got to fulfill my dream of doing something other than a desk job. I helped set up tables and decorations for special events. The Lord could not have chosen a more perfect place for me, surrounded by kind coworkers in a friendly environment. As a bonus, the church is a short commute from my home, and most of the time I get to wear my blue jeans and tennis shoes.

Since that job search experience, I've clung to Revelation 3:7 many times when making important decisions.

When it was time to buy a car, I prayed, "Lord, please close the door to any cars that are wrong for me and open the door to the right one." He led me to exactly the right vehicle—and at a bargain price, to boot.

An opportunity to travel to Italy arose. I prayed, "I'm not so sure about this overseas journey, Lord. If it's not what You want for me, please prevent my going." No hitches arose, and the trip was perfect.

My doctor recommended an elective procedure to relieve pain in my spine. But friends warned against it, citing possible dangerous complications. "God," I said, "I'm going to move forward, but if this is the wrong door for me, please shut it." Now, over two years after the procedure, I'm still enjoying relief.

As we walk closely with God, we can ask Him to protect us from bad choices and give us understanding to know which door to open. We may face trials, but His plan is always best and often leads to a place that feels right, like a favorite pair of blue jeans and tennis shoes.

Faith Step

When dilemmas arise, ask God to close opportunities that are not in your best interest, and request wisdom to recognize His will for you.

The Solid, Immutable Rock

NAN CARLTON

Jesus Christ is the same yesterday and today and forever.

—Hebrews 13:8, NIV

Mary Ethel Moore Thompson. *Mother* to her daughter. *Ethel* to her friends and extended family. *Grandma Thompson* to me. My earliest childhood remembrances of Grandma Thompson are those of an industrious, multitalented woman who doted on her family.

Depending on the season, her tireless, nimble fingers sewed church dresses of floral-print cotton, seersucker, denim, or velveteen for me. Tantalizing aromas of yeast rolls, sticky buns, and fried apple pies wafted from her kitchen, permeating every nook of her modest bungalow and making my mouth water. Endless treasures from bygone decades filled her dimly lit attic and musty basement, begging for exploration and serving to fuel my young imagination. As a child, her home was a magical space for me—a place to play and pretend and learn.

When I was twelve years old, Grandma Thompson was my Sunday school teacher. Much to her chagrin, my mind wandered incessantly at this age. I often stared out the window of our small classroom—daydreaming, contemplating anything and everything except the lesson. When this happened, my grandmother stopped talking. It was interesting how quickly complete silence grabbed the attention of this inattentive seventh grader. The two of us made brief eye contact; then she resumed the day's lesson. No fussing. No lecture about my shortcomings. Just silence, *the look*, and an offer of grace to a not-so-graceful girl in her awkward preteen years.

Not surprisingly, my childhood memories of Grandma Thompson center around what she provided for me—clothing, food, entertainment, forbearance. In youthful innocence, I supposed that hers was a worry-free life—maybe even a life that approached perfection. It would not be until my later teen years that I understood nothing could have been further from the truth.

Six years before I was born, my maternal grandfather had a left hemiplegic stroke. He never regained use of the left side of his body and was an invalid for the remainder of his life. Overnight, Grandma Thompson morphed into the role of sole breadwinner for the family. Born of necessity, she became quite frugal—a veritable penny-pincher. I can only imagine the depths of her daily struggle to exist financially, emotionally, and spiritually.

A few months after Grandpa Thompson's stroke, another family tragedy struck. My mother delivered a stillborn child. An event that everyone expected to bring much-needed joy to the family ended in broken dreams and heartache.

Grandpa Thompson died of carcinoma of the bowels six years later. I was not quite two years old at the time of his passing and do not remember him.

I knew nothing of these events when I was child. But in my youth, I took notice of infrequent grumblings—always brief, always discussed in hushed tones—concerning these tough, tragic years. Unbeknownst to my parents and grandmother, I overheard snippets of these adult conversations and was filled with questions.

Why did my grandfather die at such a young age before I could get to know him? Why was Baby William stillborn? Where was God in all this dying? Why did He let these deaths happen? How did my family keep its faith during these great losses?

As an adult, I've received answers to some of the pertinent medical questions from family members and my own research. But not all my youthful ponderings have resulted in satisfactory explanations. Many, maybe most, of my queries have gone unanswered. Despite the lack of closure concerning these crises, I gained firsthand knowledge about the mature, Christian response to life's hardships by observing the actions and words of my grandmother.

I watched Grandma Thompson through the years—always seated in the same spot on her loveseat—as she read the Bible. Frequently, she looked up from her daily reading and shared with me that this tear-stained, treasured book with the tattered cover had belonged to her father. At the end of her reading, she always closed her eyes and prayed.

On blustery, cold winter nights, oftentimes Grandma Thompson and I snuggled together before a crackling fire, munching on buttered popcorn and perusing her stuffed-to-overflowing scrapbook. My favorite items in this rather disorganized collection of memorabilia were the old photographs and a faded six-word clipping that stated, "God first. Others second. Me last." Pointing to this clipping, my grandmother always sighed deeply and whispered, "I like this." Concise, yet profound, these words were her mantra for living.

No matter if the day was as gloomy as a rainy afternoon in January or as glorious as a sun-drenched day in fall and regardless of ever-changing world events, my grandmother recited Hebrews 13:8, her favorite verse of scripture: "Jesus Christ is the same yesterday and today and forever." I listened as she made this repeated profession of faith in her unchanging Savior.

Recently, I discovered a note that Grandma Thompson penned to my parents three days after the death of Baby William. She wrote to offer some measure of comfort to my mother and father. Clearly, life was an uphill battle for my grandmother, yet her letter speaks of the joy of being reunited one day with Baby William because of their shared belief in God: "We can go to be with [Baby William] someday and spend eternity."

Through both the pleasures and the pains of life, my grandmother's temperament remained unaltered. In my early twenties, I confirmed my supposition that the source of this unwavering strength was her faith in God.

Did Grandma Thompson know that, through the years, I was intently watching and listening to her? Did she have any inkling of the impact that her words, her actions, her life of faithfulness and quiet servitude had, and continue to have, on me? I wonder.

Today, I hunger to read and study God's Word and to talk daily with Him. And I still enjoy looking at an old scrapbook and revisiting the familiar words of a beloved clipping. In the peaks and valleys of my life and in all the ho-hum landscape in between, I find myself reciting Hebrews 13:8. Mere coincidence? I think not.

To God be the glory for the godly example and legacy of my grandmother—the solid, immutable rock of our family.

Faith Step

Did family members, loved ones, or mentors instill a hunger for God's Word in you? Whether yes or no, consider how you can pass on a desire to study God's Word to future generations. What will your legacy be?

Overflowing with Assurance

LAURA BAILEY

I pray that God, the source of hope, will fill you completely with joy and peace because you trust in him. Then you will overflow with confident hope through the power of the Holy Spirit.

—Romans 15:13, NLT

My body jolted awake, and the bright red glow of the clock taunted me from across the room: 2:30 a.m. Another night, another otherwise peaceful slumber interrupted. It was useless trying to go back to sleep even though it was hours before I needed to start my day.

For the last few weeks, I've struggled going to bed and staying asleep. As much as I longed to simply lay my head on the pillow and visit with the sandman, sleep eluded me. Like clockwork, as the sun sank below the horizon and darkness took over the sky, intrusive thoughts entered my mind. I'd been contemplating my salvation, faith, and God off and on for the past few years, and I found myself in a prolonged season of spiritual unrest.

My husband, trying to help, asked me to share with him what was wrong. "Whatever it is, we can deal with it. Just tell me what is bothering you," he compassionately said one night while we were getting ready for bed. But that was the problem; it wasn't just one thing. It was hundreds, no thousands, or perhaps millions of tiny, little things. The constant stream of "What if," "Did you remember," or "What about" left me mentally, spiritually, and physically exhausted. Heightened by the lack of sleep and copious amount of caffeine consumed to help me cope, my emotions swung from barely being able to get off the couch to running circles around the house.

When I think about that time, while it is true there wasn't one particular thing I could source as the cause of my mental meltdown, there was a common theme. I was experiencing an intense season of doubt. My mind raced with questions, such as, *How can I be 100 percent certain I am saved? Why can't I feel God's presence? Is God even real?* Wrestling with my faith and experiencing doubt weren't new for me. Yet this felt different—like a full-on spiritual attack.

Over time, the anxiety and intrusive thoughts lessened but didn't go away completely. Then, one day, God used Romans 15:13 to speak to my heart, giving me the peace and assurance I'd lacked for the past few months. As a part of my morning quiet time routine, I read a daily devotional. That particular morning, the key verse was Romans 15:13. On my way to work, I always listen to the local Christian station, and the one-minute devotional covered Romans 15:13. As I read through the book our small group was studying, the author quoted Romans 15:13 as a source of encouragement when we doubt. And lastly, as I prepared for bed, a friend texted me: "I know you are wrestling right now. I pray that God fills you with joy and peace." Then she shared Romans 15:13. *OK, God! You have my attention!* I smiled as I drifted off to sleep.

Four times that day, the Lord used Romans 15:13 to calm my anxious heart. I'd heard the verse multiple times but decided to look it up in different translations. I love the New Living Translation version: "I pray that God, the source of hope, will fill you completely with joy and peace because you trust in him. Then you will overflow with confident hope through the power of the Holy Spirit." In closing his letter to the Roman church,

Paul leaves them with the beautiful reminder that not only is he praying for them but also God has the power to give our hearts and minds peace. Amen!

Paul's words struck my heart. God is a God of hope! I began to think about the meaning of hope. I use the word so conversationally that I've overlooked the true definition and ultimate weight that it holds. *I hope it doesn't rain so I can go to the game. I hope the line isn't too long so I don't have to wait. I hope everyone will get along at the holiday gathering.* And while these are all good things to hope for, they pale compared to our hope in Christ. *Hope* means "to cherish a desire with anticipation: to want something to happen or be true; trust."

My hope in the Lord leads me to trust that He is still faithful even when I can't see Him actively at work. With eager anticipation, I can wait patiently and peacefully for the Lord, looking back on the promises He has already fulfilled to assure me that He is alive and active in my life and the world. Paul reminded me and the early church that my trust in God leads me to experience the blessings of peace and joy granted by the Holy Spirit. Not on my own but through the power of the Holy Spirit, I can experience an overflowing of hope and assurance.

I wish I could say that I don't, on occasion, battle with uncertainty and doubt my salvation or God's presence or question my faith. But I've learned how to cope better, quickly shutting down thoughts I know run counter to the gospel's message. I quickly call on prayer warriors to intercede on my behalf when I'm feeling weak. I immerse myself in God's Word, committing key verses to memory to help me fight the battle that wages between my ears. I know that, more than likely, on this side of eternity, I will continue to fight these battles. But I can confidently stand firm, filled with hope, joy, peace, and assurance that I belong to the Ultimate Victor!

Faith Step

For many, the biggest battle is controlling their thoughts and emotions. Over the years, I've developed a "battle plan" for when my mind races. Do you have a plan of attack for when your thoughts begin to spiral? If not, don't delay. Make one today!

A Spirit of Youth

RAYLENE NICKEL

Bless the Lord, O my soul; and all that is within me, bless his holy name! Bless the Lord, O my soul, and forget not all his benefits, who forgives all your iniquity, who heals all your diseases, who redeems your life from the Pit, who crowns you with steadfast love and mercy, who satisfies you with good as long as you live so that your youth is renewed like the eagle's.

—Psalm 103:1–5, RSV

I sit on the grass hugging my knees, studying the face of my husband's gravestone. Every year on September 15, I come to our little country cemetery to honor the day eleven years ago when I, along with close family and friends, buried a portion of John's ashes here. The remainder I spread on a hill on our farm.

The sun's rays feel hot on my back, and the still air carries no sounds from the nearby village of Kief, North Dakota. Not far to the northeast lies our farm, its trees visible from where I sit.

Thankfully, my spirit has experienced some peace since John died. Back then, I felt as though my world had collapsed. I felt numb, hopeless, desperate. I hardly knew how to pray or what to pray for. But while thumbing through my Bible seeking comfort, I stumbled upon the words in Psalm 103:1–5. They didn't dissolve the pain, but they offered a lifeline. I thought that if I just kept praying them, some sense of order, some peace, would at last calm my spirit.

I wrote the words of the psalm on a card and buried it with John's ashes.

Now, as I sit on the grass before John's gravestone, I repeat the verses from memory. In the days, months, and years following

John's death, "Bless the Lord" had become my mantra. Over and over I repeated the words as I worked around our farm. When tasks seemed too hard, when I felt discouraged or confused, the words calmed me, reminding me that God was in control.

There was plenty to discourage and confuse me. John had died mid-stride in our farming career. After he had worked for years for a large cattle ranch, he and I had gotten started on our own farm later in life. Our finances, fields, and cattle were at last beginning to reflect sound management when John died. As a friend mused at the time, we were on a roll.

I believed I had to continue what we had started. I downsized the cow herd and began building management systems that worked for one person. I made mistakes. I experienced setbacks. Weeds increased in hayfields. Alfalfa, an important forage crop for cattle, began to thin in some fields. Disastrous winters struck, threatening the cattle-feeding systems I'd put in place. But I kept praying. I recited scripture, including Psalm 103.

Now, sitting in the cemetery, I wonder at those words in Psalm 103 promising to satisfy me with good as long as I live. Had it been good for me for John to die? Had it been good for me to struggle so hard physically on the farm? Those were hard, confusing questions. What had God had in mind by permitting those difficult circumstances?

Nevertheless, I breathe a prayer: "Thank You, Lord, that John is in heaven with You. I can't imagine his joy. And thank You for the years here for me."

God had indeed satisfied me with good, the work of my hands. The fields had rebounded with health. The cattle thrived. I paid off all our farm loans and finished buying the farm. I'd struck up a loose-knit partnership with Sam, a young neighboring farmer. And my relationship with God had deepened. I prayed for His hand to be upon every action and decision I made. Yes, I could see that He'd satisfied me with good in the years since John's death—and even long before that.

Nevertheless, in this summer of my eleventh year without John, discouragement weighed on my spirit. I felt tired. Overwhelmed. Fearful of the future. I was seventy-one. Was this what aging was all about? I rose from my bed each morning with a heavy heart. And I was beginning to dread certain tasks. Like hauling hay. As they had done every year since John died, Sam and his partners had harvested the hay on the farm. It was a record crop. My share of the hay amounted to more than two hundred 1,200-pound round bales of hay. It was more hay than I'd ever hauled from the fields into the winter feeding areas for my cattle.

I wondered if I could muster the endurance to do it—not only for me but also for my aging tractor, JD. Yes, he's a John Deere, but he's also Jesus's Disciple, hence his name. JD was a young tractor when I was a young woman. Would all of his moving parts handle the stress and strain of the work? My old hay trailer, too, would have to work extra hard. Could we all do it?

I turned to the last words in those first verses of Psalm 103: ". . . who satisfies you with good as long as you live so that your youth is renewed like the eagle's." *What does that mean?* I asked myself. *What does that kind of youth even look like?* Yes, it makes sense to me that youth will be renewed in heaven. But the words imply we can expect some measure of a renewal of youth on earth.

I started repeating the words, believing some measure of my youth can be renewed. As JD and I hauled load after load of hay up from the fields, the heavy bales balancing precariously on my old hay trailer, I repeated the verse hour after hour, day after day. I began to imagine, to see in my memory, the images of me as a young woman: strong, vigorous, courageous, willing to undertake any big task, a person who enjoyed work.

I recalled myself as a child: even though I was often filled with sadness because of the early death of my father and sometimes felt fearful of my mother, I had a child's sense of wonder. New discoveries filled me with joy, and I was excited for new events to unfold.

As I kept praying Psalm 103 and imagining my youth, my step became stronger and longer. I rose in the mornings with a lighter heart. I moved all 220 bales, and JD and I then went on to drive around the fields to bunch Sam's 450 bales into groups of eight, the number that fit perfectly on his hay trailer. That would save him the time and labor of gathering the bales himself from where they were scattered about the fields.

Perhaps the young woman I once was still lives within me and remains ever ready to offer me her strength and courage. Certainly I can trust God to bear me up on eagle's wings when life becomes difficult.

Faith Step

What qualities or strengths do you most admire in your younger self? Remember specific events when these were most evident. Believe you still possess a spirit of youth.

Trading Anxiety for His Peace

DEB WUETHRICH

"Peace I leave with you; my peace I give you. I do not give to you as the world gives. Do not let your hearts be troubled and do not be afraid."

—John 14:27, NIV

I'm not sure when I first formulated my idea of a dream job—one where I would be paid to write. It wasn't an initial thought upon entering the workforce. My husband, Gordy, and I married young. In fact, right out of high school, I accompanied him to the Michigan State University campus so he could pursue studies in agriculture. He always knew what he wanted to do. His priorities became mine. At the time, many of the campus secretaries were wives of male students, and I accepted a job in the chemistry department, which began several years of clerical work for me. The career path always put food on the table.

Gordy was in graduate school when the idea of a dream job surfaced within me, and I decided to pursue a degree. An inveterate scribbler by then, I knew I wanted to study journalism. Our young daughter's frequent illnesses cut short my curriculum at a community college, however. Michele had spinal muscular atrophy. There is no cure. Caring for her meant staying home and addressing her needs first and foremost. Priorities matter in life.

Michele passed away at the tender age of eleven, and after floundering a while, I reentered the workforce with another clerical position at a school for special education students. The job helped heal my soul since I could share our family's experience with others. One day, I looked around, wondering if it might be "my time," and resumed my studies toward a degree.

Later, when I accepted a position at a small newspaper, I realized I had finally attained dream-job status. A working reporter is paid to write news and feature stories. I developed a talent as a writer and even created a faith column for the newspaper. By this time, Gordy was well into an agricultural career as a consultant, grant writer, and adjunct professor.

But even dream jobs can have a downside. Ours was night work. Living in Southeast Michigan meant Gordy often commuted north to East Lansing to teach classes at MSU's Institute of Agricultural Technology, or south to Toledo, Ohio, to a community college. I discovered a reporter's job also meant accepting evening assignments. My beat included covering city council, school board, and area township meetings.

Gordy and I made sure whoever left the house last would leave a lamp on inside and turn on the porch light. If I was home, I anticipated the sound of the Tacoma in the drive before I could relax. (So did our one-eyed cat, Lucy, who regularly poked her head through the curtain to take a look.) I'm sure it was the same for him when the situation was reversed.

If the night shift was mine, it put me at ease to envision Gordy and Lucy tucked safely inside as I pulled in and saw the welcoming glow of lights. That is, until December 13, 2010, when Gordy experienced a massive coronary and died.

Returning to work became exceptionally difficult after that. It wasn't that I didn't want to work. I thrived on it. Work kept me occupied in life and community at a time when I almost didn't want to keep going anymore, even in a career I loved. But the loss of Gordy left me incredibly anxious. I now hated going home. Lucy often met me at the door, but she, too, seemed lost without her buddy. We both had lost a close companion.

What I most hated was the need to go out on a night assignment because it meant I would ultimately return to an empty house. True to our practice, I left a lamp on and flipped on the porch light each time I left the house. Still, entering to emptiness made me fearful and anxious. I developed a new routine. Close the door behind me, still hugging keys, purse, and tote. Turn on lights while cautiously proceeding room to room, checking to see if the back door was still locked. Peer behind shower curtains, in closets, and under the bed. Then and only then could I settle down for the night.

A palpable new fear gripped me, overriding my usual sense of security, now severely compromised. Gordy's untimely death brought new trepidation. Dread and unnamed fear replaced the happy anticipation of coming home.

One night, I approached the dark house. I'd either forgotten to turn on the porch light or it burned out. A dim glow lit the inside but didn't throw much light out a window to the doorstep. Panic hit in the dark before I even got out of the car. I knew the sad routine awaiting me as I tried to quell the uneasiness that had become my new companion.

I couldn't very well spend the night in the car. I knew what I had to do, so I took a deep breath and pushed the Toyota's door open. With racing heart, I hurried up the steps. My hands shook while poking the key in the direction of the lock. Suddenly, unexpected words rushed into my troubled mind: *Are you afraid? I will protect you.* These words calmed me instantly as I glanced into the dark night. I immediately sensed Jesus's presence and His "I am with you" promise. The door clicked open, and Lucy ran to greet me as I hit the light switch, the comfort of seeing her adding to what had just miraculously happened.

That night, I still conducted my walk-through but with a new realization. I will never be alone, in this house or anywhere.

Jesus promises a special peace—one different from what the world considers peaceful—and He says, "Do not let your hearts be troubled and do not be afraid" (John 14:27, NIV). I learned Jesus issued these words to his worried disciples as a final encouragement before the devastating trouble of His crucifixion.

Since that night, I've experienced additional confirmation to the strange encounter. Philippians 4:7 (NIV) provides a reminder of a "peace of God, which transcends all understanding" and guards hearts and minds in Christ Jesus. Isaiah 41:10 (NIV) reminds me, "Do not fear, for I am with you."

Not long after that dark night, I no longer felt the need to check every nook and cranny of my house upon coming home. When I do feel anxious, at home or anywhere else, my heart remembers a special night when God alleviated my fear in a very profound way, personally offering me His peace and protection. It is a peace the Apostle Paul points to, one accessed by faith (Romans 5:1).

Faith Step

Are you apprehensive about returning to a dark, empty house? Leave a small lamp on when you have to be away at night. Let the soft, inviting glow remind you the Spirit of God fills you—and your home—with His light and amazing love.

Wearing God's Word

STEPHANIE A. WILSEY

Now thus says the LORD, he who created you, O Jacob, he who formed you, O Israel: Do not fear, for I have redeemed you; I have called you by name; you are mine. When you pass through the waters, I will be with you, and through the rivers, they shall not overwhelm you; when you walk through fire you shall not be burned, and the flame shall not consume you.

—Isaiah 43:1–2, NRSVUE

My family and I have worn Isaiah 43:1–2 around our wrists for the past three years. A church friend, herself familiar with physical illness due to her suffering from kidney disease, ordered wristbands for us when my teenage daughter was diagnosed with a rare childhood sarcoma. These plastic wristbands are blue, my daughter's favorite color, and have Isaiah 43:1–2 stamped on them with crosses in front of and behind the Bible passage. On the reverse side is my daughter's name, Alexa, and symbols of her two passions: music and books.

We were so touched to receive these from a dear woman in the faith who knows how to encourage others through prayer and exhortation. When others struggled with how to pray over our situation, we found that sharing the blue Isaiah 43 wristbands helped them to form a prayer community around us.

Like others' cancer journeys, Alexa's started with our discovery of a mysterious lump on her leg. Unfortunately, we had trouble finding a pediatrician who would take it seriously.

Then, when we moved during the pandemic, it wasn't easy to begin with a new pediatrician. Amazingly, a pediatrician from Alexa's toddler years had switched practices to where we had moved. He immediately flagged the lump as concerning and sent us to the local children's hospital. They didn't think it was cancer but biopsied out of caution.

While on a beach in Georgia, we received the call that the lump was, in fact, cancerous. When we returned home, we immediately entered the world of scans, surgeries, and radiation. Alexa had daily treatment. She made the hour-long journey to and from the hospital with a variety of family members behind the wheel. The drivers' top responsibilities were to get Alexa there and then back to school for the afternoon while making the experience as pleasant as could be, such as by finding a quick lunch option in the city or hospital cafeteria.

By God's grace, we were up to the challenge. This is because we learned to lean into our faith deeply during this time. My parents, in-laws, husband, and brother's family had all been Christians for many decades. Alexa's diagnosis could have been a crisis of faith, but we instead drew close to the One who said that He would be with us.

My daughter said that the verse from Isaiah 43 had been her favorite Bible passage ever since hearing it quoted by a beloved teacher at her Christian middle school. I had the same teacher as a preteen, and it's particularly poignant that this teacher shared verses that later became a source of such strength and inspiration for all of us. We didn't know what the future would hold, but we knew that God would be with us. These verses didn't promise that we'd be fire- or flood-free. Rather, they promise God's presence and His intimate knowledge of us; He calls us by name.

God called Alexa's name and declared that He would be with her long before these blue wristbands declared this. She was His.

We continued to encounter this passage as Alexa's cancer journey unfolded. After her tumor was removed from her leg and radiation completed, all seemed well. But my husband and I felt unsettled. Had all the cancer been removed?

The answer was no. The following year, we learned that it had metastasized to her lungs. Others in our community asked for the blue wristbands to help remind them to pray. We started ordering bags of them and making them available to whoever wanted them. We found such encouragement in seeing the blue wristbands.

To treat the cancer, Alexa started immunotherapy. She made it through one year and then began her freshman year at college. Suddenly, the immunotherapy drug that she took daily in oral form started causing severe side effects. She experienced painful sores on her feet, hands, and mouth. Eating and walking became difficult. She found it impossible to navigate the hills of her Pennsylvania college campus.

Again, people rallied in prayer. We trusted in the God who said that we would not be consumed. Through much prayer, we decided to discontinue the medication due to toxicity and keep on the one that required monthly infusions at the hospital. We weren't sure whether the single medication would be sufficient to treat the cancer, but we felt peace over the decision.

That Christmas, Alexa's choir sang a selection from Isaiah 43. Her choir director asked Alexa to lead a devotional on the passage. She asked him if he knew that this was "her" Bible passage. He had no idea and simply assigned the verses because it was her turn.

When my family heard the piece, we all cried. We couldn't believe that we were watching Alexa sing the very words that had guided us through the past few years. She was now giving glory to the Lord for His faithfulness. Throughout that year, scans showed that her lung nodules continued to be stable; she could continue with the single drug rather than the one with the severe side effects.

As she neared the end of her two-year immunotherapy course, we traveled to Charleston, West Virginia, for a family reunion. We loved the cute town and enjoyed the coffee shops, bookstores, and libraries. Alexa noticed a reading challenge at one of the bookstores and took the sheet of paper with the instructions. Despite her busy schedule, she finished reading all the books on the challenge.

She then emailed the bookstore to say she had completed it, although she was an out-of-towner. The response was one of delight. The owner was so happy that a teen had completed the challenge and said that it was no problem that we lived far away; she'd mail the gifts shortly.

When the large box arrived, we were amazed. Not only were the gifts thoughtful and creative but also the box was filled with "You Are Mine" items emblazoned with Isaiah 43—all thematically focused on God's care.

The box arrived mere weeks before Alexa completed her treatment. Her cancer will continue to be monitored through scans, but she is no longer in active treatment. We are hopeful that God used the treatment to kick-start Alexa's immune system functioning so that she can be protected from any vestiges of cancer.

We do not know what the future holds, but we know that God will be with us and that we belong to Him.

Faith Step

Consider ways to prayerfully support others going through health crises. Whether creating bracelets or something else, concrete reminders of God's and others' love can be such an encouragement, especially when beautiful promises from God are shared.

Content with Weakness

ELIZABETH RENICKS

[The Lord] said to me, "My grace is sufficient for you, for my power is made perfect in weakness." Therefore I will boast all the more gladly of my weaknesses, so that the power of Christ may rest upon me. For the sake of Christ, then, I am content with weaknesses, insults, hardships, persecutions, and calamities. For when I am weak, then I am strong."

—2 Corinthians 12:9–10, ESV

I stood on the beach watching the surf lap the shore in a steady, pulsing rhythm. A cloudy sky hovered; surges of coastal winds whipped my hair around my face. Much of the beach was deserted on this overcast late afternoon, and I took a moment to surrender to the sounds surrounding me.

I had come to this ladies' retreat anticipating a refueling time with God, looking forward to our theme of hearing God's voice in prayer as He speaks individually to each of us. Though I was leading the teaching, I was battling to hold steady in this very area. I had arrived with a heavy heart.

The last months had been filled with emotional demands. Three friends' marriages in crisis, another friend mourning the sudden death of her husband, yet another embroiled in divisive legal proceedings with her father. I had been invited into all these hard places to pray and offer counsel. Each was seemingly spiraling out of control. I was out of answers, out of prayer energy, and out of strength.

I had come to the water's edge for a creative prayer experience called "Cast Your Sins into the Sea," modeled after an ancient Jewish custom called *Tashlich*. In that tradition, prayers are recited near natural flowing water, and one's sins are symbolically cast away when participants throw either breadcrumbs or small pebbles into the water, evoking Micah 7:19: "You will cast all our sins into the depths of the sea" (ESV). I was looking forward to casting away the burdens and sins that weighed on my weary heart.

Shifting my gaze from the waves to the laminated bookmark in my hand, I read the instructions for this prayer time. I was to pick up a handful of rocks or shells, then spend some time talking with God about the sins or burdens in my life. The instructions continued: "One by one, cast your rocks and shells into the water, naming each one for a sin or burden you would like the Lord to carry away. Confess. Cast. Praise. Worship. Repeat."

Putting the bookmark under a pile of sand, I gathered a handful of items from the beach. I walked closer to the water and started naming and throwing.

"I confess to you my pride," I prayed aloud, and pitched my rock out into the surf, watching it sink away beneath the foam. I could feel the release of confession. I had been trying not only to bear my friends' burdens but also to fix them all through my own wisdom, wanting to be seen as a reliable and helpful minister to hurting ones.

I continued, naming and throwing sins and burdens. I began to feel lighter as, one by one, I watched rocks sink beneath the surface. I worked down my mental list of things to cast away, getting louder and bolder with each throw.

"I give you my weakness," I shouted over the noise of the surf, throwing out the next item in my hand. I watched it land. But this rock did not disappear. Instead, it floated and started making its way back toward me.

I was puzzled and not amused. I wanted to be rid of weakness perhaps more than any other thing I had come to the shore to cast away. I wanted God's sea of forgiveness and cleansing to take weakness as far from me as the east is from the west.

Frustrated that I hadn't gotten to watch that one sink, I walked down the shore a few feet to get away from the weakness and finish my prayers. But that little thing I had just thrown into the water was still floating atop the waves, coming right toward me. Annoyed and a little spooked, I moved again. *How is a rock floating?* I wondered as I walked more quickly down the shoreline.

I looked back. It had followed me again. Annoyed, I stopped and watched as the "rock" I had thrown into the surf made its way toward my feet.

I sensed God telling me to go pick it up. Reluctantly, I stepped into the water and scooped up what I had thought I was getting rid of. Obviously, God had other ideas.

As I grasped the item and pulled my hand up out of the water, I realized I was holding a little round nut of some sort, cracked, and obviously too light to have sunk. I hadn't noticed that everything I picked up from the beach was not a rock.

I had tried to throw away my weakness, and God had sent it right back to me.

All at once I saw clearly. God did not view my weaknesses as either a sin or as something He wanted to take away from me. He sent that weakness nut right back to me with a very strong impression in my spirit: "Your weaknesses are where I can do the best work."

I knew about Paul. I knew the verse about God's power being made perfect in weakness (2 Corinthians 12:9). But standing on the shore and holding that little nut in my hand, I began to recognize that God wasn't messing around about the truth Paul penned: "For when I am weak, then I am strong" (2 Corinthians 12:10, ESV).

God got my attention that day about seeing my weaknesses in the proper light—not as something to be rid of but as an offering to Him. Weakness is a gateway to grace and power beyond what I could imagine. Little did I know, standing on the beach, that in the next years, God would allow me to face challenges that would dwarf those that had so wearied me coming into that retreat.

But God knew, and He was making me ready by showing me that His grace is sufficient and His power is made perfect in weaknesses. He knew that in the next years I would navigate the emotions of my younger brother having open heart surgery at age forty-three. He knew two months later He would call me to care for my mother as she was diagnosed with an aggressive cancer that took her life within a year. He knew that a year after her death, there would be a pandemic that shut down the whole world and would layer global fear and division on top of my deep grief. God knew, too, that during those years, I would also shepherd my teenage son through two lung collapses and two surgeries. He knew about all the places I would feel overwhelmed and fragile. He knew the places where I would be tempted to give into fear and to give up on hope.

Through all those experiences, the little weakness nut I brought home from the beach that day sat in a place of honor in my prayer closet. I saw it daily and was tangibly reminded of the simple truths of God's Word and His heart. It is a truth best summed up in a line from "Jesus Loves Me": "Little ones to Him belong. They are weak, but He is strong."

Faith Step

Reflect on your own thoughts about weakness. Do you view it as something you need to be rid of? Or as a sin? Invite God to give you His strength in all the places you are currently feeling weak, depleted, uncertain, or overwhelmed.

Finding Safety

REBECCA HASTINGS

I lift up my eyes to the mountains—where does my help come from? My help comes from the LORD, the Maker of heaven and earth. He will not let your foot slip—he who watches over you will not slumber; indeed, he who watches over Israel will neither slumber nor sleep. The LORD watches over you—the LORD is your shade at your right hand; the sun will not harm you by day, nor the moon by night. The LORD will keep you from all harm—he will watch over your life; the LORD will watch over your coming and going both now and forevermore.

—Psalm 121, NIV

On a beautiful September day, I left the cute little house my husband and I rented near the beach. Throwing on some shorts, a T-shirt, and a pair of sneakers, I was going to help a friend and then head to class. I was a senior in college. I drove down the windy road, the sun shining and the radio on. It was 9:30 in the morning, and the day was going to be beautiful.

Until everything around me was still. My car wasn't moving, nothing seemed to be moving. I opened my eyes wondering where I was. Looking down to the right I saw my rearview mirror on the floor. *That's not where that goes.* Pain took over my body, and all I could do was scream. This was not just any scream. This scream was from a place I hadn't known existed; primal and loud, it became white noise, the background to all that had happened.

Someone tried to open my door, and it was jammed. I sat alone in my car, bleeding and screaming. My screams mixed with tears as a woman opened the passenger door. She had a cool washcloth in hand and began wiping my face. I still wonder where it came from, that washcloth. Perhaps it was from the house with the front-row seat to the events of that morning. It is one of many things I'll never know. The woman was telling me it was OK, that I was OK. Everything felt so far from OK. I uttered two things over and over:

I passed out.
Call my husband.

The woman called my husband for me, telling him I had been in a little accident. I still remember those words: *little accident.* There was nothing little about crashing head-on at fifty miles per hour. My tiny hatchback was no match for the Lincoln Continental, and I had no airbags. I never knew my face could bend a steering wheel, but it did. The scars are hidden in my mouth, and I still feel them when the weather turns.

Firefighters came, and the memories are in staccato segments like a slideshow. The firefighter covering my body and face with his coat. *Click.* The deafening sound of the Jaws of Life. *Click.* Glass shattering. *Click.* Voices talking all around me, maneuvering me, strapping me down, covering my wounds. *Click.* And just as they lifted me out of the car, my husband's voice, "I'm here, I'm here." And finally, I could stop screaming.

The police waited outside the trauma room at the hospital as doctors, nurses, and family came and went. The uniformed officer stood, unmoving outside the door wanting answers. So did I. I didn't understand what happened. One minute I was driving on a beautiful day, and the next I was in pain and bleeding. When I was stable, the doctors let the officer in, and he asked his questions, probing me for answers that would make this simple.

Where were you going? *To class.*
What time did you leave? *Around 9 a.m.*

What did you have for breakfast? *Cereal.*

What did you drink with that cereal? *Orange juice.*

Are you sure? Was there something in that orange juice? *It was just juice.*

So what happened? *I blacked out while I was driving.*

Let's try this again.... Was there anything in your juice?

I'd never felt so confused. I wanted answers as much as they did, probably more. This wasn't just an incident file for me; this was my life. And someone else's. I had hit someone else. Oh my God. I hit someone else. And, yes, I thought, *Oh my God.* Not *oh my* or *oh my goodness.* God was the only one who could handle this. This was all my fault. But I didn't mean to do any of it.

Discharged the same day with more stitches than I could count, a chipped bone, and pain, I went home to heal and understand. Healing came. Understanding took longer. I felt like my body had betrayed me. I felt fragile and scared.

In the days following the accident, I saw doctor after doctor, looking for answers. After a few weeks, we found two: I was diagnosed with epilepsy and vasovagal syncope, both of which can cause me to pass out. I thought the answers would help, but they only brought more questions, and one kept flashing in my mind again and again: *Will I ever be safe?*

Even as I started medication and made plans with the doctors, I wondered if the fear inside me would ever go away. I caused an accident. Thankfully, the other driver only had minor injuries, but my body was untrustworthy.

Little by little, I talked to God. I told Him how scared I was. I told Him how sorry I was. And I asked Him the question that plagued me. If I couldn't trust myself, my own body, the only thing I had left to trust was God.

Scholars believe David wrote Psalm 121, both as a cry to God and a declaration of God's protection. As I read these words, they became my prayer, a place for me both to cry out with my deepest fears and declare God's promises over my life. After some time without my license, I went back to driving. Each time filled me with fear, but then I remembered Psalm 121. I prayed it; I declared it over my fear. As God's truth wove its way around my heart and mind, I found safety in His faithfulness.

Change didn't come overnight. Sometimes, I find myself gripping my steering wheel, fears of the past creeping in. But I know I don't have to stay in that fear. I can come to God again, confident that He is faithful. Psalm 121 reminds me of who God is: more than my fear, more than what I can control. I may not know what every circumstance holds, but God is the place for me to keep finding safety.

Faith Step

Whenever you struggle with fear or anxiety, read Psalm 121 aloud and declare God's faithfulness over you and your life.

Where the Good Is

SUE MCCUSKER

This is what the LORD says: "Stand at the crossroads and look; ask for the ancient paths, ask where the good way is, and walk in it, and you will find rest for your souls."

—Jeremiah 6:16, NIV

Storms circled around me as I stood shaking uncontrollably in the basement of our home. We had been through so much over the last year, and now tornadoes threatened my family and our house. I huddled in the corner of my Georgia home and listened to the howling winds swirl outside at 2 a.m., the day after Easter. Usually, I'm calm and levelheaded, always offering hope, but this time, I was shaken to my core.

My mind raced as I thought about all the events that led up to this. We had just finished celebrating an unusually quiet Easter at home this year. Our world was in the middle of a historic pandemic. The stock market crashed due to the uncertainty, and my husband received news of potential layoffs at his job. In addition, we had been talking about retiring soon. I had always relied on my dad's steady and reassuring voice in times like this, but his passing a year earlier had left only silence. So when the storms came this time, my faith was rattled.

"Where are you going?" my husband asked as I retreated to the corner of the basement. I did not want my family to see me upset. They were much calmer than I was and continued watching the approaching storm on television with an up-to-the-minute forecast. But for me, it had become overwhelming.

I felt small and helpless against circumstances I did not understand and could no longer control. Alone in the corner,

I began to pray. I prayed through the shaking and the sobs. I prayed through the roaring winds outside that sounded like a freight train. But no matter how hard I prayed, I could not stop shaking.

Finally, the winds subsided outside. Although we escaped the storm this time with minor damage, it left me feeling tired and defeated. The following day, I stepped outside to pick up the branches scattered around the yard. "Thank You, Lord," I managed to say. I was genuinely thankful the storm had bypassed us, but I could not shake my gloomy feeling. I was exhausted, and the days dragged on without focus or purpose. I was constantly checking forecasts for reassurance. Even my morning coffee ritual did not provide its usual pick-me-up.

The spring storms eventually gave way to warmer weather, and my husband's job had worked out after all, but I was not feeling any better. I let out a heavy sigh one morning as I stood in the kitchen, filling the coffee pot with water and trying to jump-start my day. I didn't know what else to do but to tell God exactly how I felt. *I'm going to put it all out on the table*, I thought, *no sugarcoating or pretending*.

"Lord, I'm tired," seemed like a good place to start as I began my conversation with God that morning. I wasn't in the mood for grand prayers anyway, and I believe God likes it when we are honest with Him. Every morning after that, I began by telling God how I was feeling while I made my morning coffee. Then I would sit down and search the pages of scripture for comfort.

As I poured out my tears to God one morning, a particular passage in the Bible stood out to me. It was from Jeremiah 6:16: "Stand at the crossroads and look; ask for the ancient paths, ask where the good way is, and walk in it, and you will find rest for your souls."

Jeremiah was a prophet known for crying out to God. He lamented over the state of Jerusalem and the troubles the people were going through. How fitting this was for me! I, too, cried out to God. Jeremiah's words resonated with me. "This is what the Lord says to do," he often wrote, repeating the phrase for extra emphasis. I decided to give it a try.

"God, show me where the good way is," I asked. I know God's ways are good, and He has forged a path for us from the beginning of creation, but I cannot see it now. "Show me what is good, so I can walk in it," I continued to pray.

Over the next few days, I began to notice things differently when I came downstairs to the kitchen to prepare my morning coffee and get ready for the day. I opened the pantry door to reach for the bag of coffee, and I saw shelves full of food. A feeling of gratitude suddenly swept over me as I realized we had enough food to eat during these times without worry. I poured a cup of coffee and sat at the dining room table. The steam rose from the mug and warmed my hands on this brisk morning. The aroma of freshly brewed coffee calmed my senses and invited me to sit awhile. Rays of golden sunshine streamed through the windows and lit up the room. I gazed out the window and saw trees standing tall and strong after the storms, their beauty reaching toward the sky. God's ancient paths were evident in His creation.

Then I looked around my house and felt an immense thankfulness for the comfortable home that held so many beautiful memories. The table where I'd cried out to God was also where I held my newborn son years ago. It is where grandparents had gathered, sharing laughter and prayers over plates of delicious food. Many family dinners were served at this table too. We labored over schoolwork and rested here at the end of the day. My family, although a little older now, was still sleeping upstairs in this early morning hour, safe and warm in their beds. We were healthy, and we were together.

God had shown me the good way through the storm! I smiled as I realized God had shown me what was good right here in my home. I regained my joy and strength that day. Now, I enjoy the simple blessings of appreciating everyday life. Storms still come and go in my life, but I have peace knowing I can always go to God with whatever I am feeling, and He will patiently listen over endless cups of coffee. God will always show me the good way. I only need to ask.

Faith Step

Ask God to show you the good way in your life. Start a morning routine by talking to God and telling Him how you feel. Look for encouragement in your Bible, and then follow God's good path.

Where Your Treasure Is

JENNIE IVEY

"Lay not up for yourselves treasures upon earth, where moth and rust doth corrupt, and where thieves break through and steal. . . . For where your treasure is, there will your heart be also."

—Matthew 6:19, 21, KJV

I looked around my small, new-to-me house and marveled at its emptiness. There was no furniture in any of the rooms. Nothing in the kitchen cabinets. Nothing in the closets. Nothing in the basement or garage or attic. And the house was clean. Very clean. Fresh paint on the walls. New carpet in the bedrooms. Gleaming tile in the bathroom. Sunshine flooded through windows so recently washed it seemed as if there was no glass in them at all.

If this was what a fresh start looked like, I was totally on board.

For thirty-five years, I'd lived with a husband who often seemed to be more in love with his stuff than he was with me. He'd grown up poor and struggled to pay his way through school. But once he began working as a physician, the shopping and spending began. Year after year, it escalated.

To put it mildly, we lived in a cluttered environment. Our garages (there were several) were filled with cars and motorcycles and boats and bicycles and sports equipment. His woodworking shop was jam-packed with tools. A large shed housed a zero-turn lawnmower and other landscaping equipment. We even had a home gymnasium. He rented a hangar at a regional airport for his vintage plane and a slip at a boat dock for his vintage houseboat. Our spacious house overflowed with TVs, stereo equipment, computers, and other electronics. Expensive paintings hung on the walls. Closets overflowed with clothes and shoes, most of them his.

It was all too much. Too much to take care of. Too much to pay for. (Yeah, we were in debt. Big time.) And far too much to use, especially by someone whose job required working long hours with little time off. We argued about all that stuff. A lot.

"I'm the breadwinner," he told me. "I can do what I want with my money. I've never denied you or the kids anything you want or need. Someday soon," he insisted, "I'll have time to enjoy all these things I've bought."

I could only shake my head in despair. Our three children had arrived in quick succession not long after we married. He loved them deeply and still does. But his work and his hobbies often kept him from being fully present, physically and emotionally. He attended the kids' ballgames and piano recitals and awards ceremonies when his on-call schedule allowed.

But "religion" was my responsibility. Though he begrudgingly bowed his head at the dinner table while one of the children said the "God Is Great" blessing, he rarely attended church with us. Sunday morning, he declared, was the perfect time to make hospital rounds.

I envied families who attended worship services with both parents present. I envied wives in my "couples" Sunday school class who sat with their husbands' arm resting lightly on the chair behind them. I envied those who went together to Wednesday evening supper and Bible study. But that wasn't my life. Not at all. The kids and I read Bible stories together when they were little. I encouraged them to participate in church music programs and youth group. We worked together on service projects. When it came to passing my faith along to my kids, I did my best. But I'd always felt like a single mom.

Years passed. The kids grew up and flew the nest. And my husband and I grew further and further apart. He took up golf. When he wasn't at the hospital, he spent a lot of time partying at the airport or the lake. Or riding motorcycles with his buddies. Or sitting in front of his computer, shopping. Soon after he turned sixty, he decided that, instead of more stuff, what he really wanted was a girlfriend.

That's how I ended up, alone for the first time in my life, in this totally empty house. How would I fill it? One thing was certain. It wouldn't be with stuff.

I was determined not to load my things willy-nilly into a rented trailer. Prayerfully and deliberately, I made a list of what I would take from the house my husband and I had shared for so many years. Pictures of our children, though I left him half of them. My late mother's oak dining table. My grandmother's cast-iron skillet, blackened with age and use. A beloved aunt's rocking chair. I donated most of my clothes and shoes to a thrift shop. I separated my many books into "give away" and "keep" piles. Among those books was my great-grandmother's well-worn, red-letter King James Bible. How long had it been since I'd opened that Bible and read it? Too long. My eyes welled up with tears as I hugged it to my chest. The Bible wouldn't go into a box with my other books. It would travel to my new house beside me on the seat of my car.

There's no pretending that the end of my long marriage was anything but horrible. It was one of the most painful things I've ever been through. The divorce itself was bitter and contentious. And while it dragged on and on, I learned just how little I knew about how a house works. Or how a car works. But as time passed, I developed new skills. How to drive a nail and change out a furnace filter. How to check oil levels and tire pressure. A whole lot of other stuff too. Most importantly, I learned that though my kids were sad, they still loved both me and their dad as much as ever.

Slowly but surely, I figured out how to fill the empty spaces in both my house and my life. I took time to think. To write. To listen. To pray. My new home held only the things I needed and loved. I created a bunk room in the basement where the kids and grandkids could sleep when they came to visit. I had dishes and chairs enough to host summer cookouts and winter soup suppers for my friends. A big plant stand near my sunny windows. A cozy reading chair and a sturdy bookshelf in my living room.

I don't keep my well-worn, red-letter King James Bible on that bookshelf. It rests, instead, on the lamp table beside my chair. Seeing it reminds me to pick it up and read it. I've taken to keeping a fine-point ink pen tucked inside that Bible so I can mark passages that are important to me, just as my great-grandmother did.

One of her favorite verses is mine too. In the sixth chapter of Matthew, Jesus reminds us that "where your treasure is, there will your heart be also." Yes, Lord, yes.

Faith Step

Take time to go through the place where you live and get rid of things you no longer need or love. Give thanks for the items you kept and for the blessed empty space you've created.

Wisdom for Senior Living

KAREN LUKE HESS

Teach us to number our days, that we may gain a heart of wisdom.

—Psalm 90:12, NIV

Life looks different after sixty. I have no idea how many more days are ahead of me, but certainly there are more days in the rearview mirror than on the horizon. I'm thankful for my good health, but I've had enough little reminders that my body isn't what it used to be to realize the importance of being intentional about taking care of myself. More of my calendar is devoted to doctor appointments, but I certainly don't feel old yet. For years I've said that I don't really want to grow old; I just want to be young for a long, long time. Now that my husband and I have been empty nesters for a number of years, I'm putting more thought into the purpose of this season. I don't want to look back in twenty years and realize I've wasted this precious gift of time. How do I want this season of life to look? And, perhaps more importantly, what does the Lord expect of me?

While feeling unsure about how to become more intentional about not squandering the days I do have, I began by posting a dedicated calendar in a prominent place (on my bathroom wall) to remind me that life is short. To add focus, I wrote, "Teach me to number my days, that I may gain a heart of wisdom" on a sticky note that I move around as I cross off the days. Consequently, most mornings and evenings while brushing my teeth, I reread those words as a mini-prayer. Easy enough. To my delight, I discovered that taking this little step of faith has been effective and powerful. A good reminder that the Lord is always pleased to answer when we ask Him for wisdom.

Without my even recognizing it at first, the Lord began helping me to reevaluate my passions and to set goals. My days feel significant when I include my priorities: faith, fitness, family, friends, finances (posted inside my medicine cabinet). Using this wisdom, lunches with friends, which often tempted me to overeat and overspend, transitioned to walking dates. Together we get some exercise, enjoy being outdoors, and stay caught up on each other's lives. Eventually, I set more intentional goals, for example, praying for each family member and personal VIPs regularly, visiting with each local grandchild weekly, visiting more distant grandchildren monthly, and donating a box of rarely used items monthly. These simple habits began to give me the structure and filters I needed to help me stay focused on what is most important to me.

Long ago, a mentor taught me that as we grow in the Christian life, our temptations transition too. Giving in to the temptation of the good can rob us of what is best. Perhaps more than anything else, I truly long to leave a significant legacy of godly living to my grandchildren. If I regularly choose shallow activities over after-school time with my grandchildren, I will miss out on getting to know them deeply; learning about their gifts, troubles, and joys; and praying with them and for them in meaningful ways. Precious memories shared with these little ones remind me that these vital relationships grow best bit by bit, week by week, not just at holiday gatherings or family vacations. In response to their curiosity, I've had the pleasure of explaining how God created the world and each of them, the difference between weeds and flowers, and how the rock cycle works. I've also heard about great school days and really hard ones. How can these precious moments begin to compare with browsing in a thrift shop or reading one more chapter of a novel?

Early in my Christian walk, I tried to incorporate every new teaching into my life immediately. It took me years to internalize the idea of seasons of life. I spent lots of years feeling guilty and burdened by all that was undone and assuming the Lord was not any happier with me than I was with myself. No more. Finally, I know the Lord isn't a harsh taskmaster. Now, to me, that's real wisdom in real time. He appreciates my time and desire to serve him by serving my family, friends, and community. He also knows I need to take care of myself. (That's the thing about self-care—you can't delegate it!) Knowing this has allowed me to be more relaxed about how often I write in my journal and read my Bible and offer prayers—but also to be more mindful of how I use my time. Day by day, I am learning to lean into the wisdom the Lord gives me.

Being calmer in my approach is clarifying some themes that align with my spiritual gifts and passions. As I have the opportunity, I press into these areas and walk away from (or politely decline) other invitations. For now, my themes are the following: grandparenting, prayer, leadership, and science. My hobbies are loom knitting, gardening, and hiking. As I focus on these areas, little confirmations come my way: an invitation to a prayer seminar, a thrift-shop find (a student microscope), an opportunity to knit hats for a mission project. I feel blessed to be guided toward and sometimes away from what grabs my attention. Believing that the Lord loves me a great deal and cares about how I spend my days has resulted in my becoming a better steward of my time each day. But I still wanted more guidance.

Eventually, I discovered a Bible passage that has become like a treasured recipe: "Make every effort to add to your faith goodness; and to your goodness, knowledge; and to knowledge, self-control; and to self-control, perseverance, and to perseverance, godliness; and to godliness, mutual affection; and to mutual affection, love. For if you possess these qualities in increasing measure, they will keep you from being ineffective and unproductive in your knowledge of our Lord Jesus Christ" (2 Peter 1:5–8, NIV). I know that following this template will enrich my senior years and keep me from being ineffective and unproductive as I travel through this rich season of life. Hallelujah!

Faith Step

Hang up a wall calendar with the words of Psalm 90:12 written on a sticky note to open up new avenues of spiritual growth and wisdom.

Writing on His Hand

TERRIE TODD

"But for now, dear servant Jacob, listen—yes, you, Israel, my personal choice. GOD who made you has something to say to you; the God who formed you in the womb wants to help you. Don't be afraid, dear servant Jacob, Jeshurun, the one I chose. For I will pour water on the thirsty ground and send streams coursing through the parched earth. I will pour my Spirit into your descendants and my blessing on your children. They shall sprout like grass on the prairie, like willows alongside creeks. This one will say, 'I am GOD's,' and another will go by the name Jacob; That one will write on his hand 'GOD's property'—and be proud to be called Israel."

—Isaiah 44:1-5, MSG

Christian parents of adult children who've wandered from faith know how it feels to weep over their kids. They're not alone. Books, videos, and podcasts from Christian publishers, organizations, and leaders populate the top ten lists in parenting. These resources offer help and encouragement to parents whose hearts are broken because their offspring do not love Jesus the way they'd hoped and dreamed.

Somehow, I didn't think much about this when our three kids were little in the eighties and nineties. My husband and I were raised in Christian homes. Though our families of origin certainly weren't without their share of troubles, each member of our generation hung on to their faith. When I think of family gatherings at my parents' home, for example, I know Mom could have asked any one of us to lead in prayer before a meal. We could have and would have done so without feeling ill at ease.

(I use this "saying grace" example as a weak measuring stick only. I realize it's quite possible to offer a fake, unfelt prayer.)

If I thought about this at all back then, I assumed our experience would be similar when our turn arrived to don the grandparenting cloak. After all, we attended church and Sunday school every week. We said prayers at meals and bedtime. Bible stories were read and verses memorized. We placed our kids in a Christian school. If anything, they'd be far better equipped for life than we had been. I naturally anticipated happy gatherings where we could share faith stories, pray, and worship together as a family. Though geographical distance would mean we attended different churches, all would attend somewhere. And when we did gather, we'd attend together.

I thought.

So it's been a shock—as it has to many Christian parents—to realize the outcome I hoped for didn't automatically follow. Issues I'd never dreamed we'd face have driven us to our knees and evoked tears beyond counting. I couldn't have imagined then that any of our children would choose to live their lives without God.

I'm grateful for those who have walked this road and offered advice. I've received much encouragement from others. No matter the length of their books, videos, or studies, the bottom line tends to boil down to this: as Christian parents of adult children, our role is to keep praying, listening, supporting, and shutting our mouths unless asked to speak. Of course, the interpretation of those things is varied and puzzling. We can't go wrong asking for God's wisdom to define what support looks or sounds like.

One day I sat pouring my heart out before God for my kids, especially our youngest. A talented tattoo artist by profession, he appears to have no use for God, church, or prayer. While I wouldn't use the word *estranged*, we see him only a couple of times a year and always by our initiative.

"Lord," I prayed, "I know You love him even more than we do. You understand his heart far better than we ever will. You desire a relationship with him, but You'll never force him against his will." As I wept, I picked up my Bible and asked God to give me a scripture to let me know our son would be OK—maybe not today, but in God's timing—whatever OK means to God. I recognized that my definition of OK may not match my Heavenly Father's. This is part of the letting-go process we parents must walk through.

I'm not usually one to open my Bible randomly, but this time I did. It fell open to Isaiah 44. Here's what I read: "God who made you has something to say to you; the God who formed you in the womb wants to help you."

The Lord certainly grabbed my attention with this introduction. "What do you want to tell me, God?" I asked before eagerly reading on.

"Don't be afraid, dear servant. . . . I will pour my Spirit into your descendants and my blessing on your children."

"Wow. Really, God?" I could scarcely believe what I read, having chosen this so randomly after praying so specifically. I kept going.

"They shall sprout like grass on the prairie, like willows alongside creeks."

That resonated with me too. We live on the prairies, and the property on which we raised our children is peppered with willows. A river even runs alongside it. My heart began to beat faster as I knew for certain God was speaking directly to me, even though these ancient words were originally spoken to the Israelites. I kept going.

"This one will say, 'I am GOD's,' and another will go by the name Jacob; That one will write on his hand 'GOD's property'—and be proud to be called Israel."

By now, I was sobbing. The phrase "That one will write on his hand" slayed me. God knew exactly what I needed. He assured me I could trust Him with my tattoo artist son, whose hands may be the only part of his body not already "written on."

I printed out the passage and kept it within view.

Twelve years have passed since that day. I wish I could report answered prayer in the form of changed lives, my children walking with God and serving Him with their whole hearts. I cannot. If anything, the intervening years have brought deeper grief. I know the next twelve may bring still more. But none of that makes this scripture passage any less true. Time means nothing to God. If a thousand years are as a day to Him, then twelve years, twenty years, forty years are nothing. His promises to me will unfold in His time. His Word is good. I can rest on His assurances as I anticipate the day I'll see His perfect plan realized. The longer I must wait, the greater the joy will be.

Faith Step

Have you been praying for decades for your children to return to God? Has your faith been challenged in a whole new way? As you continue to pray, ask God to use this in your life—to keep you humble, to keep you listening, and to keep you on your knees.

A Mom Next Door

MEADOW RUE MERRILL

God places the lonely in families.

—Psalm 68:6, NLT

Eight months pregnant, I stood by the front window of our century-old fixer-upper, feeling weary and overwhelmed. My husband, Dana, and I had been married for sixteen years and cherished our four children, including our adopted daughter, Ruth, who had cerebral palsy. Each child was a blessing. But our budget was thin and my energy low.

"God," I prayed that gray January day, staring past the neighboring houses and down our icy city street, "I need more grandparents for my children."

Dana's mom lovingly knitted beautiful sweaters and mittens for our children and brought books and treats on birthdays. And his dad had once given us a van when we'd outgrown our sedan. But they lived an hour up the coast. My own mom lived in Connecticut, three states away. My dad had left when I was four, and my only sibling, a brother, lived in Hawaii, leaving me largely alone.

When I was growing up, my family had felt small. Too small. That was one reason I craved a big, bustling family of my own. My mother loved me, but as a single parent she was often preoccupied with paying the bills. Soon after I'd left for Bible school at seventeen, she'd rented out our house and went back to school herself, spending much of the following two decades overseas. My mom was many things—independent, adventurous, filled with a love for God, for which I am incredibly grateful. But she was also often absent.

So with just a few weeks left before this baby's arrival, I was feeling overwhelmed. "I should post a help-wanted ad in the paper," I joked to Dana that evening. "Grandparents wanted."

Later that week, I was standing in the kitchen, trying to figure out what to make for dinner, when the phone rang. It was my neighbor Joan, who lived a few houses up the block and ran the local candy store. "Don't make dinner," she said. "I'm on my way over."

I hung up the phone and rubbed my aching back, remembering the gingerbread houses Joan had baked for our children just before Christmas, complete with bowls of gumdrops and bags of sugary icing. What was she up to now?

"Mom, come look out the window!" twelve-year-old Judah exclaimed from the living room a few minutes later.

Squeezing around the counter with my swollen belly, I waddled into the next room, where Judah and his younger siblings crowded around the frosted window where I'd prayed mere days before. Looking over their silky heads, I gasped. There, marching down the slick sidewalk in their winter boots, came Joan, followed by her husband, Paul. Each carried a large cardboard box. As they crossed the road and clambered up our stairs, I swung open the door, letting in a gust of frigid air.

"What's this?" I asked, banging the door closed behind them.

Stomping off the snow, Joan and Paul headed straight for the kitchen.

"Chicken cacciatore," Joan said. Sliding her box onto the counter, she pulled out a foil-wrapped pan. "Meat loaf." She lifted out another. "Mashed potatoes. Chicken and broccoli. Chicken noodle soup. Salad. Brownies. Ice cream. Fudge sauce. Root beer." As the children and I gaped in astonishment, Joan presented one dish after another.

When the boxes were finally empty, my counter was covered. "I know how tired and busy you must be," said Joan, who had also raised five children. "So I made enough food for a week."

Joan fed our family that night—and for many nights thereafter. But that wasn't all. When our son Asher arrived three weeks later, she became "Grammy Joan," baking five blue-and-white frosted cakes for his baby shower, each decorated with a letter of his name. She took our children for sleepovers so Dana and I could spend time together. She filled our house with gifts at Christmas. She grieved with us the following winter when Ruth unexpectedly passed away in her sleep. She brought Asher to work with her at the candy shop so I could rest. And she celebrated the birth of our youngest child, Ezra, with us two years later.

Just after Ezra turned one, my mom was stricken with a fast-moving cancer. Joan took the kids, made meals, and offered to help as I drove eight hours round trip to care for her. My mom died just before Christmas. A few weeks later, my family and I drove wearily home from Connecticut after my mother's funeral. When I stepped into our kitchen, I found a steaming Crock-Pot of chili simmering on our counter, along with a plate of corn muffins and a card. From Joan, of course.

Born five years apart, my mom and Joan could not have been more different. One a hippie farmer turned globe-trotter. The other a businesswoman turned chocolatier. So imagine my surprise when I discovered that Joan and my mom shared the same birthday. As if God, knowing how much I would one day need a mom next door, had planned from the very beginning to send us one more grandparent.

Psalm 68:6 says, "God places the lonely in families" (NLT). Or as the King James Version says, "the solitary." It is not just those who feel alone that God cares for. It is those who are on their own. Those who have no one. And He does it through us. Such love might begin with a phone call. Or a meal. Or a knock on a neighbor's door, the way God used Joan. All it takes is a caring heart and a willingness to get involved.

In the fifteen years since God's unexpected answer to my prayer, Paul passed away and both of our families moved. Joan, to a cozy condo. We, to a fixer-upper in the country. We now live thirty minutes away, but Joan is still a daily part of our lives. Mailing care packages as our older children have left home. Molding chocolate lobsters for Judah's wedding. Picking up our younger children from school when I can't. Dropping off meals. And sending frequent texts to let me know that she is praying for me.

So this past year, when Dana and I began the process to become licensed foster parents to care for two young children from our church in need of a home, Joan was the first person I called.

"What can I do to help?" she asked.

"Nothing," I said, thinking of all the love Joan has poured into our family over the years. "You taught me how to help when others need a hand."

Faith Step

If you feel lonely, ask God to show you someone else who may also feel alone. Then reach out with a phone call, a card, or an invitation for a meal. You just may be the answer to someone else's prayer.

Acknowledgments

Every attempt has been made to credit the sources of copyrighted material used in this book. If any such acknowledgment has been inadvertently omitted or miscredited, receipt of such information would be appreciated.

Scripture quotations marked (ESV) are taken from the *Holy Bible, English Standard Version*. Copyright © 2001 by Crossway Bibles, a division of Good News Publishers. Used by permission. All rights reserved.

Scripture quotations marked (KJV) are taken from the *King James Version of the Bible*.

Scripture quotations marked (MSG) are taken from *The Message*. Copyright © 1993, 2002, 2018 by Eugene H. Peterson.

Scripture quotations marked (NASB and NASB1995) are taken from the *New American Standard Bible*. Copyright © 1960, 1962, 1963, 1968, 1971, 1972, 1973, 1975, 1977, 1995 by The Lockman Foundation, La Habra, California. Used by permission.

Scripture quotations marked (NIV) are taken from *The Holy Bible, New International Version*. Copyright © 1973, 1978, 1984, 2011 by Biblica, Inc. Used by permission of Zondervan. All rights reserved worldwide. zondervan.com

Scripture quotations marked (NKJV) are taken from *The Holy Bible, New King James Version*. Copyright © 1982 by Thomas Nelson.

Scripture quotations marked (NLT) are taken from the *Holy Bible, New Living Translation*. Copyright © 1996, 2004, 2007 by Tyndale House Foundation. Used by permission of Tyndale House Publishers Inc., Carol Stream, Illinois. All rights reserved.

Scripture quotations marked (NRSVUE) are taken from *New Revised Standard Version, Updated Edition.* Copyright © 2021 by National Council of Churches of Christ in the United States of America. Used by permission. All rights reserved worldwide.

Scripture quotations marked (RSV) are taken from the *Revised Standard Version of the Bible*, copyright © 1946, 1952, and 1971 by the Division of Christian Education of the National Council of the Churches of Christ in the United States of America. Used by permission. All rights reserved.

A Note from the Editors

We hope you enjoyed *Living the Word*, published by Guideposts. For over 75 years, Guideposts, a nonprofit organization, has been driven by a vision of a world filled with hope. We aspire to be the voice of a trusted friend, a friend who makes you feel more hopeful and connected.

By making a purchase from Guideposts, you join our community in touching millions of lives, inspiring them to believe that all things are possible through faith, hope, and prayer. Your continued support allows us to provide uplifting resources to those in need. Whether through our communities, websites, apps, or publications, we inspire our audiences, bring them together, and comfort, uplift, entertain, and guide them. Visit us at guideposts.org to learn more.

We would love to hear from you. Write us at Guideposts, P.O. Box 5815, Harlan, Iowa 51593, or call us at (800) 932-2145. Did you love *Living the Word*? Leave a review for this product on guideposts.org/shop. Your feedback helps others in our community find relevant products.

Find inspiration, find faith, find Guideposts.
Shop our best sellers and favorites at
guideposts.org/shop
Or scan the QR code to go directly to our Shop.